Japanese for Fun

Japanese for Fun

Make Your Stay
in Japan More Enjoyable.

Taeko Kamiya

TUTTLE PUBLISHING
Tokyo • Rutland, Vermont • Singapore

Published by Tuttle Publishing, an imprint of Periplus Editions,
with editorial offices at 130 Joo Seng Road, #06-01 Singapore 368357
and 364 Innovation Drive, North Clarendon, Vermont 05759.

LCC Card No. 89-51718
ISBN-10: 4-8053-0866-4
ISBN-13: 978-4-8053-0866-0

Distributed by:

North America, Latin America and Europe
Tuttle Publishing
364 Innovation Drive,
North Clarendon, VT 05759-9436, USA
Tel: (802) 773 8930
Fax: (802) 773 6993
E-mail: info@tuttlepublishing.com
www.tuttlepublishing.com

Japan
Tuttle Publishing
Yaekari Building, 3rd Floor,
5-4-12 Osaki, Shinagawa-ku,
Tokyo 141-0032
Tel: (03) 5437 0171
Fax: (03) 5437 0755
E-mail: tuttle-sales@gol.com

Asia Pacific
Berkeley Books Pte Ltd,
130 Joo Seng Road #06-01/03,
Singapore 368357
Tel: (65) 6280 1330
Fax: (65) 6280 6290
E-mail: inquiries@periplus.com.sg
www.periplus.com

09 08 07 06
8 7 6 5 4 3 2 1

Printed in Singapore

Contents

Foreword

This pocket book is intended for people who want to learn Japanese quickly. Whenever you have a few free minutes—waiting in a hotel lobby, riding on a train, or wherever—open this book and you can learn phrases you'll use again and again during your stay in Japan. The book is divided into twenty-one chapters, each covering a specific topic. Each chapter includes the following three sections.

Words & Expressions: This section introduces words and expressions needed in specific situations. Vocabulary is presented systematically for quick and easy understanding.

Expressions in Context: This shows how to use in context the words and expressions given in the preceding section. Gives you confidence in using new words in original sentences.

Additional Words & Expressions: This section enables you to create many new sentences using the patterns just learned. There's no need to memorize all the words or phrases presented here; concentrate on just those you want to use.

Start by reading the first three chapters of the book. These introduce many of the most commonly used words and phrases, and familiarize you with the basic sentence structures. After Chapter 3, go straight to any chapter that interests you. If you want to know what to say on the phone, read Chapter 14; if you have to take a train, a few minutes with Chapter 6 should enable you to reach your destinaton quickly and conveniently.

Altogether, this book contains over three hundred carefully selected words and expressions. There is very little grammar included and there is no need for hours of rote memorization. All that is required is a few minutes of your time.

One final word of advice. Do not be afraid to use what you learn. Only by taking the initiative and speaking out can you experience the joy of communicating in a foreign language. With this new method, you'll discover how fun and easy speaking Japanese can be.

Taeko Kamiya

Pronunciation

VOWELS

The Japanese language has five vowels: **a, i, u, e,** and **o**. The vowels are pronounced as follows:

a as in f*a*ther
i as in *e*at
u as in r*u*le
e as in m*e*t
o as in s*o*lo

In spoken Japanese, the **i** and **u** vowel sounds are often weak. This occurs in words like **shika** (deer), which may sound like **shka**, or **desu**, which may sound like **dess**.

Long vowels are pronounced twice as long as regular vowels and are marked **ā, ii** or **ī, ū, ē** and **ō**. In this book the double **ii** is used instead of a macron.

CONSONANTS

Most Japanese consonants are pronounced like English consonants. One exception is the Japanese **r**, which sounds like a combination of the English **r** and **l**.

As shown in the following table, each consonant is followed by a vowel, by a **y** and a vowel, or by an **h** and a vowel. Each syllable is clearly pronounced; thus **haru** (spring) is **ha-ru**; **kyaku** (customer) is **kya-ku**; and **shumi** (hobby) is **shu-mi**.

When **n** is followed by a vowel within a word, an apostrophe is used to show the break between syllables. Examples of this include **kin'en** (nonsmoking) and **man'in** (no vacancy).

Double consonants (**kk, pp, ss, tt**) are pronounced as follows: **Nikko** (famous tourist spot) like the **k** sound in "book-keeper"; **rippa** (fine) like the **p** sound in "top part"; **issō** (more) like the **s** sound in "less sleep"; **kitte** (stamp) like the **t** sound in "hot tub."

Following is a table of all the sounds in Japanese. It is recommended that you practice the sounds aloud at least two or three times.

TABLE OF SOUNDS IN JAPANESE

a	i	u	e	o
ka	ki	ku	ke	ko
ga	gi	gu	ge	go
sa	shi	su	se	so
za	ji	zu	ze	zo
ta	chi	tsu	te	to
tsa*	ti*	tu*	tse*	tso*
da	di*	du*/dyu*	de	do
na	ni	nu	ne	no
ha	hi	fu	he	ho
ba	bi	bu	be	bo
pa	pi	pu	pe	po
fa*	fi*	—	fe*	fo*
ma	mi	mu	me	mo
ya	—	yu	—	yo
ra	ri	ru	re	ro
wa	—	—	—	—
n	—	—	—	—
kya	—	kyu	—	kyo
gya	—	gyu	—	gyo
sha	—	shu	she*	sho
ja	—	ju	je*	jo
cha	—	chu	che*	cho
nya	—	nyu	—	nyo

hya	—	**hyu/fyu***	—	**hyo**
bya	—	**byu**	—	**byo**
pya	—	**pyu**	—	**pyo**
mya	—	**myu**	—	**myo**
rya	—	**ryu**	—	**ryo**

* These sounds are used only in loanwords, words derived from other languages.

A Word About Japanese Grammar

It is not the purpose of this book to explain Japanese grammar. However, it is probably worthwhile to point out a few basic differences between Japanese and English.

1. Japanese verbs come at the end of a sentence.
   Ex. **Watashi wa biiru o <u>nomimahss</u>.** (I <u>drink</u> beer.)

2. Japanese nouns generally do not have plural forms. The noun **kodomo**, for example, can mean either "child" or "children."

3. Articles and some common English adjectives are not used in Japanese. There are no Japanese equivalents for words like "a," "the," "some," and "any."

4. The subject of a sentence, especially **watashi** (I) and **anata** (you), is often dropped.

5. The same verb form is used for both the present and future tenses.
   Ex. **Watashi wa ikimahss.** (I go./I will go.)

6. Three important Japanese particles have no equivalents in English.
   Wa follows the topic or subject of a sentence.
      Ex. **Watashi wa Honda dess.** (I am Honda.)
   Ga follows the subject of a sentence.
      Ex. **Hoteru ga arimahss.** (There is a hotel.)
   O follows the direct object of a verb.
      Ex. **Biiru o nomimahss.** (I drink beer.)

7. Adding the word **ka** to the end of a sentence makes it a question.
   Ex. **Kore wa hoteru dess ka?** (Is this a hotel?)

CHAPTER 1
Basic Expressions

You'll use these basic expressions again and again during your stay in Japan. If you can, practice them aloud. It'll take you only a few moments to learn them, and when you do, you'll have taken the first and most important step to speaking Japanese.

WORDS & EXPRESSIONS

Ohayō gozaimahss.	Good morning.
Konnichiwa.	Hello./Good afternoon.
Konbanwa.	Good evening.
Oyasumi-nasai.	Good night.
Sayōnara.	Goodbye.
Jā mata.	See you later.
Omedetō gozaimahss.	Congratulations.
Dōmo arigatō.	Thank you.
Dō-itashimashite.	You're welcome.
O-genki dess ka?	How are you?
o-	(honorific prefix)
genki	healthy; fine
hai	yes
iie	no
Hai, genki dess.	(Yes,) I'm fine.
Hajimemashite.	How do you do? (used only when you are introduced to someone)
Dōzo yoroshiku.	Glad to meet you.
O-namae wa?	What's your name?
O-shigoto wa?	What's your occupation?
Wakarimahss.	I understand.

Wakarimasen.	I don't understand.
Nihon-go	Japanese (language)
Nihon-go wa wakarimasen.	I don't understand Japanese.
Nihon-go ga heta dess.	My Japanese is poor.
Sumimasen.	Excuse me.
Honda-san	Mr./Mrs./Ms./Miss Honda
-san	(honorific added to another person's name; not used with your own name)
Ei-go	English
Ei-go ga wakarimahss ka?	Do you understand English?

HOW TO BOW

Bowing properly takes practice, and many companies, especially hotels and department stores, spend considerable time training new employees to do it correctly. The secret to good bowing? Keep your back straight and bend from the hip. Your feet should be placed together and your hands at your sides or clasped in front. Bow deliberately, without rushing. If you don't know what to say as you bow, say **Dōmo**, a phrase that's appropriate for most occasions. One exception is when you're paying respects to the decreased. In that case, just keep silent.

EXPRESSIONS IN CONTEXT

Honda-san, konnichiwa.	Good afternoon, Mr. Honda.
Sumisu-san, konnichiwa.	Good afternoon, Mrs. Smith.
Sumisu-san, ohayō gozaimahss.	Good morning, Mr. Smith.
Sumisu-san, konbanwa.	Good evening, Miss Smith.
O-genki dess ka?	How are you?
Hai, genki dess.	(Yes,) I'm fine.
Hajimemashite. Honda dess.	How do you do? I'm Honda.
Dōzo yoroshiku.	I'm glad to meet you.

Hajimemashite. Sumisu dess.	How do you do? I'm Smith.
Dōzo yoroshiku.	I'm pleased to meet you.
Omedetō gozaimahss.	Congratulations!
Dōmo arigatō.	Thank you.
Dō-itashimashite.	You're welcome.
Jā mata.	See you later.
Sayōnara.	Goodbye.
Oyasumi-nasai.	Good night.

ADDITIONAL WORDS & EXPRESSIONS

Wakarimahss ka?	Do you understand?
Hai, wakarimahss.	Yes, I understand.
Iie, wakarimasen.	No, I don't understand.
Mō ichido itte kudasai.	Please say it once more.
Ei-go de hanashite kudasai.	Please speak in English.
yukkuri	slowly
Yukkuri hanashite kudasai.	Please speak slowly.

LANGUAGES

Betonamu-go	Vietnamese
Chūgoku-go	Chinese
Doitsu-go	German
Furansu-go	French
Indoneshia-go	Indonesian
Itaria-go	Italian
Kankoku-go	Korean
Porutogaru-go	Portuguese
Roshia-go	Russian
Supein-go	Spanish
Tai-go	Thai

CHAPTER 2
What's What

Over half of what we say in English is made up of fewer than fifty words. It's the same in Japanese. Just by learning the following words and phrases, you'll be able to make hundreds of different sentences. And remember, to make a question, add **-ka** to the end of a sentence.

WORDS & EXPRESSIONS

kore	this
wa	(subject particle)
jinja	Shinto shrine
dess	is; am; are
Kore wa jinja dess.	This is a Shinto shrine.
are	that
o-tera	Buddhist temple
o-	(honorific prefix)
Are wa o-tera dess.	That is a Buddhist temple.
Kabuki-za	the Kabuki Theater
kabuki	Kabuki
Are wa Kabuki-za dess ka?	Is that the Kabuki Theater?
hai	yes
sō dess	that's right
Hai, sō dess.	Yes, it is.
iie	no
dewa arimasen	isn't; am not; aren't
hanga	woodblock print
Kore wa hanga dewa arimasen.	This isn't a woodblock print.
nan(i)	what

Kore wa nan dess ka?	What's this?
torii	Shinto shrine archway
Torii dess.	This is a Shinto shrine archway.
Kōkyo	the Imperial Palace
Kore wa Kōkyo dess ka?	Is this the Imperial Palace?
o-shiro	castle
Are wa o-shiro dess ka?	Is that a castle?
bonsai	miniature potted tree or shrub
Kore wa bonsai dess.	This is a *bonsai*.
fūrin	wind chime
Are wa fūrin dewa arimasen.	That isn't a wind chime.

SHRINES AND TEMPLES

What's the difference between a shrine and a temple? Shrines are worship grounds for Shinto, a religion that originated in Japan. Temples are worship grounds for Buddhism, which originally came from India. In many places in Japan, shrines and temples stand side by side.

A shrine can be identified by a **torii**, an arch made of two crossbeams supported by two pillars. The **torii** represents the union of man and woman and marks the entrance to the shrine grounds. At a temple, you can always find a statue of a buddha inside one of the buildings.

EXPRESSIONS IN CONTEXT

Kore wa nan dess ka?	What's this?
O-tera dess.	This is a Buddhist temple.
Kore wa jinja dess.	This is a Shinto shrine.
Kore wa torii dess.	This is a Shinto shrine archway.
Are wa nan dess ka?	What's that?
Are wa Kabuki-za dess.	That's the Kabuki Theater.

Are wa Kōkyo dess.	That's the Imperial Palace.
Are wa o-shiro dess.	That's a castle.
Kore wa hanga dess ka?	Is this a woodblock print?
Hai, sō dess.	Yes, it is.
Iie, hanga dewa arimasen.	No, it's not a woodblock print.
Kore wa bonsai dess ka?	Is this a *bonsai*?
Hai, sō dess.	Yes, it is.
Iie, bonsai dewa arimasen.	No, it's not a *bonsai*.
Are wa fūrin dess ka?	Is that a wind chime?
Iie, fūrin dewa arimasen.	No, it isn't a wind chime.

GEOGRAPHICAL TERMS

yama	mountain
heiya	plain; open field
kawa	river
mizuumi	lake
umi	ocean
Taihei-yō	Pacific Ocean
Seto-naikai	Inland Sea
ken	prefecture
Hiroshima Ken	Hiroshima Prefecture

SIGHTSEEING

machi	town; city
inaka	country; rural area
tō	pagoda; tower
butsuzō	statue of a buddha
sanmon	temple gate
hakubutsu-kan	museum

bijutsu-kan	art museum
dōbutsu-en	zoo
shokubutsu-en	botanical garden
yūen-chi	amusement park
Ueno Kōen	Ueno Park
eki	station
Tōkyō Eki	Tokyo Station
Tōkyō Tawā	Tokyo Tower
Teikoku Hoteru	Imperial Hotel
cha-batake	tea field
kaki-yōshokujō	oyster bed (cultivated)
suiden	rice paddy

AROUND TOWN

dōro	road
kōsoku-dōro	expressway
michi	street
biru	building
kōsō-biru	skyscraper
hoteru	hotel

CHAPTER 3
Introducing Yourself

Polite speech in Japanese, which is very complicated, is based on being respectful when referring to others and humble when referring to yourself. Don't worry about polite speech too much though. Just remember to attach **-san** to other people's names and to not use it with yours.

WORDS & EXPRESSIONS

watashi	I
Sumisu	Smith
dess	is; am; are
Watashi wa Sumisu dess.	My name is Smith. (*lit.,* I'm Smith.)
Amerika-jin	American (person)
Watashi wa Amerika-jin dess.	I'm an American.
anata	you
Tanaka-san	Mr./Mrs./Ms./Miss Tanaka
ka	(question particle)
Anata wa Tanaka-san dess ka?	Are you Mr. Tanaka?
Sō dess.	That's right.
Chigaimahss.	No, I'm not.
dewa arimasen	isn't; am not; are not
Nihon-jin	Japanese (person)
ano	that
hito	person
ano hito	that person
dare	who
Ano hito wa dare dess ka?	Who's that person?
watashi no	my

chichi	father (one's own father)
Watashi no chichi dess.	He's my father.
Tanaka-san no	Mr./Mrs./Ms./Miss Tanaka's
otōsan	father (someone else's father; also used when addressing one's own father)
Tanaka-san no otōsan dess.	He's Mrs. Tanaka's father.
anata no	your
namae	name
Anata no namae wa?	What's your name?

POLITE COMPLICATIONS

Many new employees spend their first days on the job learning when to use honorific and humble speech. It can be confusing at first. For example, suppose a new employee is talking to the company president. He'll be using as many honorifics as he can. The phone rings. The young man picks it up but it's for the president. "He's in" the young man says using humble speech to refer to his president. Rude? Far from it. He's merely showing respect to the caller, someone outside his company, by using humble speech to refer to a member of his own company, even if that person's status is much higher than his.

EXPRESSIONS IN CONTEXT

Ano hito wa dare dess ka?	Who's that person?
Tanaka-san dess.	That's Mr. Tanaka.
Watashi wa Sumisu dess.	My name is Smith.
Watashi wa Amerika-jin dess.	I'm an American.
Anata wa Sùmisu-san dess ka?	Are you Miss Smith?
Hai, sō dess.	Yes, I'm.
Iie, chigaimahss.	No, I'm not.
Anata wa Amerika-jin dess ka?	Are you an American?

Anata wa Nihon-jin dess ka?	Are you Japanese?
Ano hito wa Tanaka-san no otōsan dess ka?	Is that person Mrs. Tanaka's father?
Watashi wa Nihon-jin dewa arimasen.	I'm not Japanese.
Ano hito wa Tanaka-san dewa arimasen.	That person isn't Mr. Tanaka.
Ano hito wa watashi no chichi dewa arimasen.	That person isn't my father.
Anata no namae wa?	What's your name?
Sumisu dess.	My name is Smith.

NATIONS AND NATIONALITIES

Amerika	United States
Betonamu	Vietnam
Betonamu-jin	Vietnamese
Chūgoku	China
Chūgoku-jin	Chinese
Furansu	France
Furansu-jin	French
Igirisu	England
Igirisu-jin	English
Itaria	Italy
Itaria-jin	Italian
Kanada	Canada
Kanada-jin	Canadian
Kankoku	Korea (ROK)
Kankoku-jin	Korean
Doitsu	Germany
Doitsu-jin	German

Ōsutoraria	Australia
Ōsutoraria-jin	Australian
Porutogaru	Portugal
Porutogaru-jin	Portuguese
Roshia	Russia
Roshia-jin	Russian
Supein	Spain
Supein-jin	Spanish

OCCUPATIONS

sensei	teacher
gakusei	student
hisho	secretary
kaisha-in	company employee
bengo-shi	lawyer
kisha	reporter; journalist

RELATIVES

haha	mother (one's own mother)
okāsan	mother (someone else's mother, and when addressing one's own mother)
ani	older brother (one's own older brother)
oniisan	older brother (someone else's older brother, and when addressing one's own older brother)
ane	older sister (one's own older sister)
onēsan	older sister (someone else's older sister, and when addressing one's own older sister)

otōto	younger brother (one's own younger brother)
otōto-san	younger brother (someone else's younger brother)
imōto	younger sister (one's own younger sister)
imōto-san	younger sister (someone else's younger sister)
musuko	son (one's own son)
musuko-san	son (someone else's son)
musume	daughter (one's own daughter)
musume-san	daughter (someone else's daughter)
mago	grandchild (one's own grandchild)
o-mago-san	grandchild (someone else's grandchild)

OTHERS

tomodachi	friend
kare	he
kanojo	she
kodomo	child
otona	adult
onna	female
otoko	male
onna no ko	girl
otoko no ko	boy
onna no hito	woman
otoko no hito	man

CHAPTER 4
Asking Directions

With one word, **sumimasen**, you can ask a stranger a question, get a store clerk's atten-
tion, and apologize for just about anything. On top of that, you can use **sumimasen** to
express thanks for a kind act; for example, when someone gives you directions or offers
you something to drink.

WORDS & EXPRESSIONS

Sumimasen.	Excuse me.
takushii-noriba	taxi stand
doko	where
Takushii-noriba wa doko dess ka?	Where's a taxi stand?
asoko	over there; that place
Asoko dess.	It's over there.
koko	here; this place
Koko wa doko dess ka?	Were am I?/Where's this place?
eki	station
tōi	far
Eki wa tōi dess ka?	Is the station far?
chikai	near
Iie, chikai dess.	No, it's near.
Shinjuku	Shinjuku (place name in Tokyo)
chizu	map
chizu de	on the map
Shinjuku wa chizu de doko dess ka?	Where on the map is Shinjuku?
o-tearai	restroom
O-tearai wa doko dess ka?	Where's the restroom?
soba	near

erebētā	elevator
Erebētā no soba dess.	It's near the elevator.
kusuri-ya	pharmacy
koko massugu	straight ahead
Kusuri-ya wa koko massugu dess ka?	Is the pharmacy straight ahead?
mae	in front
Hai, eki no mae dess.	Yes, it's in front of the station.

SPEAKING ENGLISH IN JAPAN

What to do when your Japanese fails you? Speak in English. English-speaking people abound in Japan—the trick is knowing who and how to ask. Your best bet lies with young businessmen, professional working women, and high school and college students. Many students, having spent years studying English, would love the chance to talk with you.

Still, when confronted by a foreigner, some Japanese may be so surprised that their hearing and speaking ability fail. Speak slowly and clearly. If that fails, try writing down what you want on paper.

EXPRESSIONS IN CONTEXT

O-tearai wa doko dess ka?	Where's a restroom?
Erebētā wa doko dess ka?	Where's an elevator?
Shinjuku wa tōi dess ka?	Is Shinjuku far?
Hai, tōi dess.	Yes, it's far.
Iie, chikai dess.	No, it's near.
Eki wa chizu de doko dess ka?	Where on the map is the station?
Koko dess.	Here it is.
Kusuri-ya wa eki no mae dess.	The phrmacy is in front of the station.
O-tearai wa erebētā no soba dess.	The restroom is near the elevator.
Takushii-noriba wa koko massugu dess.	The taxi stand is straight ahead.
Sumimasen. Koko wa doko dess ka?	Excuse me. Where am I?

Shinjuku dess.	In Shinjuku.
Eki wa chikai dess ka?	Is the station near?
Hai, asoko dess.	Yes, it's over there.

PLACES

kūkō	airport
basu-tei	bus stop
chika-tetsu no eki	subway station
chūsha-jō	parking lot
gasorin-sutando	gas station
kyōkai	church
taishi-kan	embassy
ryōji-kan	consulate
ginkō	bank
yūbin-kyoku	post office
mise	store
depāto	department store
hon-ya	bookstore
kamera-ya	camera shop
pan-ya	bakery
gifuto-shoppu	gift shop
kissa-ten	coffee shop
keisatsu-sho	police station
kōban	police box

WITHIN A BUILDING

esukarētā	escalator
kaidan	stairs
kai	floor

Nan-kai dess ka?	What floor?
Ni-kai dess.	The second floor.
uketsuke	reception desk
naka	in; inside
soto	out; outside
chika	basement
okujō	roof
iriguchi	entrance
deguchi	exit

DIRECTIONS

higashi	east
nishi	west
kita	north
minami	south
ushiro	behind
ue	up
shita	down
migi	right
hidari	left

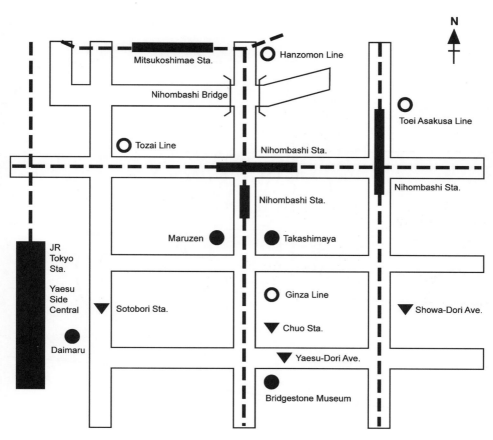

Nihombashi

CHAPTER 5
Numbers

For counting ten objects or less, use the numbers presented below. For example, if you want six rolls of film, say **Firumu, muttsu kudasai**. If you have four baggage pieces, say **Ni-motsu ga yottsu arimahss**. The good thing about numbers is that you can always use your fingers to make certain someone understands you.

WORDS & EXPRESSIONS

hitotsu	one
kudasai	please; please give
Hitotsu kudasai.	Please give me one.
kore	this
Kore, hitotsu kudasai.	Please give me one of this.
sandoitchi	sandwich
futatsu	two
Sandoitchi, futatsu kudasai.	Please give me two sandwiches.
firumu	film
mittsu	three
Firumu, mittsu kudasai.	Please give me three rolls of film.
yottsu	four
itsutsu	five
muttsu	six
nanatsu	seven
yattsu	eight
kokonotsu	nine
tō	ten
ikutsu	how many
Ikutsu dess ka?	How many are there?/How many do you want?

Tō dess.	There are ten./I want ten.
nimotsu	bag; baggage
ga	(subject particle)
arimahss	there is; there are
Nimotsu ga ikutsu arimahss ka?	How many bags are there?
Yottsu arimahss.	There are four.
takusan	many
Takusan arimahss.	There are many.

COUNTERS

Another way of counting uses special words that are attached to numerals. These words, called counters, vary according to the type of object. For example, long, thin objects like pens take the counter **hon**; flat objects use **mai**.

Counters exist for cars, fish, birds, buildings, airplanes, clothing, small animals, and large animals. There's even one for Japanese poems, and a different one for Chinese poems. But don't fret about remembering all of them. It's all right to count things with **hitotsu, futatsu, mittsu**, etc.

EXPRESSIONS IN CONTEXT

Sumimasen. Kore, kudasai.	Excuse me. Please give me this.
Ikutsu dess ka?	How many do you want?
Tō, kudasai.	Ten, please.
Kore, futatsu kudasai.	Please give me two of these.
Kore, muttsu kudasai.	Please give me six of these.
Sandoitchi, yottsu kudasai.	Please give me four sandwiches.
Firumu, mittsu kudasai.	Please give me three rolls of film.
Firumu, itsutsu kudasai.	Please give me five rolls of film.
Nimotsu ga ikutsu arimahss ka?	How many bags are there?
Nanatsu arimahss.	There are seven.

Kokonotsu arimahss.	There are nine.
Firumu ga takusan arimahss ka?	Do you have many rolls of film?
Hai, yattsu arimahss.	Yes, I have eight.
Iie, hitotsu arimahss.	No, I have one.

NUMBERS

The numbers presented here are used for time, prices, rankings, and so forth. These numbers may also be used for counting more than ten objects.

ichi	1
ni	2
san	3
shi/yon	4
go	5
roku	6
shichi/nana	7
hachi	8
ku/kyū	9
jū	10
jū-ichi	11
jū-ni	12
jū-san	13
jū-shi/jū-yon	14
jū-go	15
jū-roku	16
jū-shichi/jū-nana	17
jū-hachi	18
jū-ku/jū-kyū	19
ni-jū	20

ni-jū-ichi	21
san-jū	30
san-jū-ichi	31
yon-jū	40
go-jū	50
roku-jū	60
shichi-jū/nana-jū	70
hachi-jū	80
kyū-jū	90
hyaku	100
hyaku-ichi	101
hyaku-jū	110
ni-hyaku	200
san-byaku	300
yon-hyaku	400
go-hyaku	500
rop-pyaku	600
nana-hyaku	700
hap-pyaku	800
kyū-hyaku	900
sen	1,000
san-zen	3,000
has-sen	8,000
ichi-man	10,000
san-man	30,000
jū-man	100,000
hyaku-man	1,000,000
Firumu, jū-san kudasai.	Please give me thirteen rolls of film.
Kore, ni-jū kudasai.	Please give me twenty of these.

COUNTING PEOPLE

hitori	1 person
futari	2 people
-nin	(suffix used for counting more than two people)
san-nin	3 people
yo-nin	4 people
go-nin	5 people
roku-nin	6 people
shichi-nin/nana-nin	7 people
hachi-nin	8 people
kyū-nin/ku-nin	9 people
jū-nin	10 people
Hito ga go-nin imahss.	There are five people.
otoko no hito	man
onna no hito	woman

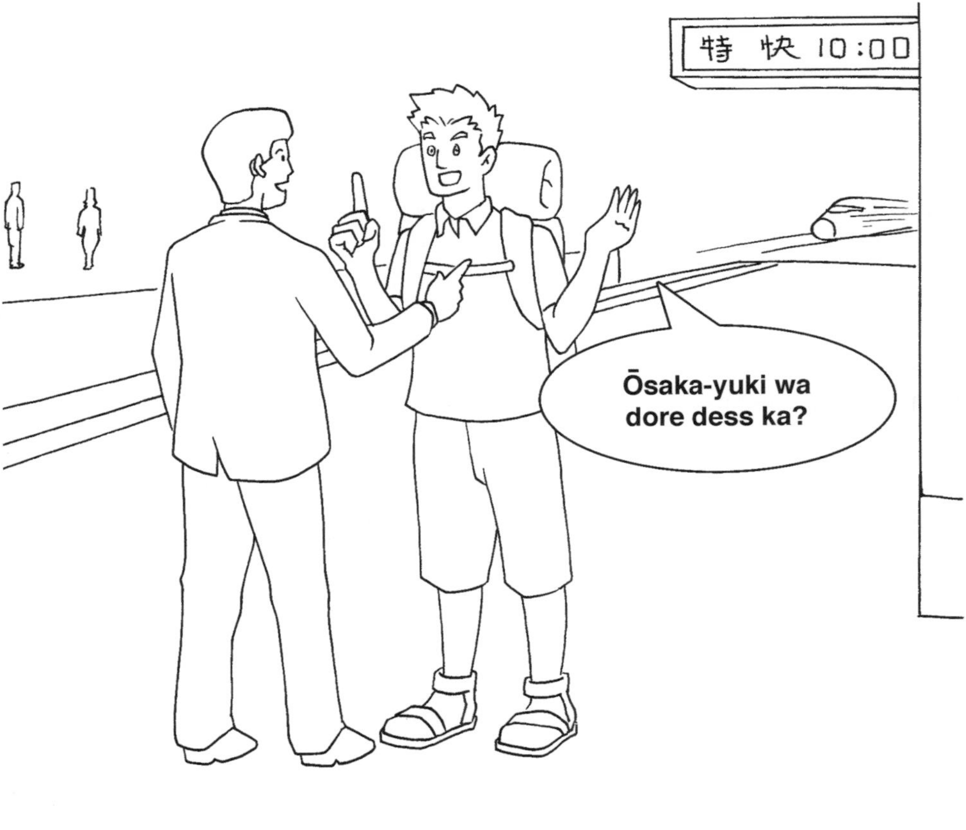
特快 10:00
Ōsaka-yuki wa
dore dess ka?

CHAPTER 6
Taking the Train

If you don't know which train ticket to buy, ask a station employee (or a kind-looking stranger). Or buy the cheapest ticket and pay the remainder when you get off. Make sure you ask which platform to use and which train to take; some trains don't stop at every station.

WORDS & EXPRESSIONS

kono	this
densha	train
kono densha	this train
Ōsaka	Osaka
e	(particle indicating direction)
Ōsaka e	to Osaka
ikimahss	go
Kono densha wa Ōsaka e ikimahss ka?	Does this train go to Osaka?
ikimasen	doesn't go / don't go
Iie, ikimasen.	No, it doesn't go.
-yuki	bound for ~
Ōsaka-yuki	bound for Osaka
dore	which one
Ōsaka-yuki wa dore dess ka?	Which one is bound for Osaka?
are	that one
Are dess.	That one is.
kippu	ticket
ikura	how much
Kippu wa ikura dess ka?	How much is the ticket?
Kyōto	Kyoto

Kyōto made	to Kyoto; as far as Kyoto
Kyōto made, ikura dess ka?	How much is it to Kyoto?
Roppongi	Roppongi (place name in Tokyo)
Roppongi made, ikura dess ka?	How much is it to Roppongi?
dono	which
hōmu	platform
Dono hōmu dess ka?	Which platform is it?
san-ban	# 3
san-ban hōmu	platform # 3
San-ban hōmu dess.	It's platform # 3.

JAPAN'S TRAINS

Japan has perhaps the best train and subway system in the world. Not only are trains safe, clean, and efficient, they traverse practically every part of Japan. The Japan Railways Group (JR), which owns eighty percent of Japan's rail system, offers a handy, economical rail pass. With this pass, you can ride throughout Japan on JR trains (including the bullet trains) as well as on JR buses and ferries. Ask your travel agent how to purchase the pass before you leave your home country because you cannot buy it in Japan.

EXPRESSIONS IN CONTEXT

Sumimasen. Kono densha wa Ōsaka e ikimahss ka?	Excuse me. Does this train go to Osaka?
Hai, ikimahss.	Yes, it does.
Iie, ikimasen.	No, it doesn't.
Kyōto-yuki wa dore dess ka?	Which one is bound for Kyoto?
Roppongi-yuki wa are dess ka?	Is that one bound for Roppongi?
Tōkyō-yuki wa dono hōmu dess ka?	Which platform does the train bound for Tokyo leave from?

Kippu wa ikura dess ka?	How much is the ticket?
Ōsaka made, ikura dess ka?	How much is it to Osaka?
Tōkyō made, ikura dess ka?	How much is it to Tokyo?
Sumimasen. Kyōto-yuki wa are dess ka?	Excuse me. Is that one bound for Kyoto?
Iie. Yon-ban hōmu dess.	No. It leaves from platform # 4.
Iie. Ōsaka-yuki dess.	No. It is bound for Osaka.

TYPES OF TRAINS

Shinkansen	bullet train
tokkyū	limited express
kyūkō	express
futsū	local train
chika-tetsu	subway

AT THE STATION

te-nimotsu ichiji azukari-jo	baggage checkroom
kiosuku; eki no baiten	kiosk, newspaper stand, station shop
machiai-shitsu	waiting room
rokkā	locker
annai-jo	information office
unchin-hyō	fare table
jikoku-hyō	timetable
(kippu no) jidō-hanbaiki	ticket machine
kaisatsu-guchi	wicket; ticket gate
katamichi(-kippu)	one-way (ticket)
ōfuku(-kippu)	round-trip (ticket)
zaseki shitei-ken	reserved-seat ticket

ON THE PLATFORM

-gō-sha	car # ~
ni-gō-sha	car # 2
~ -ban-sen	track # ~
Nan-ban-sen dess ka?	Which track # is it?
San-ban-sen dess	It's track # 3
kin'en-sha	nonsmoking car
jiyū-seki	nonreserved seat
shitei-seki	reserved seat
Jiyū-seki wa nan-gō-sha dess ka?	Which cars have non-reserved seats?
shokudō-sha	dining car
eki-ben	box lunch sold at stations or on trains
akabō	redcap; porter
shashō	conductor
eki-in	station employee
nori-kae	transfer
Chūō-sen	Chuo line (train line from Tokyo to Nagano Prefecture)
-sen	line (train)
Tōkyō Eki de nori-kae dess ka?	Do I transfer at Tokyo Station?
Hai, Chūō-sen ni nori-kae dess.	Yes, you transfer to the Chuo line.
Chikatetsu ni nori-kae dess.	You transfer to the subway.

CHAPTER 7
Buses and Taxis

If you can't find taxis on the street, you can usually get them at designated areas near train stations. Empty taxis display a red light; full ones, a green light. Try to have the address of your destination written in Japanese; this can be very helpful when riding taxis or buses.

WORDS & EXPRESSIONS

Ginza	Ginza (place in Tokyo)
made	to; as far as
Ginza made	to Ginza
itte kudasai	please go
Ginza made itte kudasai.	Please go to Ginza.
migi e	to the right
magatte kudasai	please turn
Migi e magatte kudasai.	Please turn to the right.
hidari e	to the left
ano	that
kado	corner
ano kado de	at that corner
tomete kudasai	please stop (a car)
Ano kado de tomete kudasai.	Please stop at that corner.
toranku	trunk (of a car)
o	(direct object particle)
Toranku o akete kudasai.	Please open the trunk.
Kanda	Kanda (place name in Tokyo)
ni tomarimahss	stop at
basu	bus

Kono basu wa Kanda ni tomarimahss ka?	Does this bus stop at Kanda?
koko	here
tsuitara	when we get there
oshiete kudasai	please tell
Tsuitara, oshiete kudasai.	When we get there, please tell me.
ikura	how much
Ikura dess ka?	How much is it?
sen-en satsu	1,000-yen note
kuzushite kudasai	please break (into change)
Sen-en satsu, kuzushite kudasai.	Please break this 1,000-yen note.

BUSES

In major cities, you usually pay a flat fee for riding a bus. Sometimes you pay when you get on, sometimes when you get off.

In smaller cities and rural areas, you usually pay according to the distance traveled. As you get on, look for a machine that automatically gives you a ticket with a number on it. This ticket, which indicates where you got on the bus, determines your fare. Hand over the ticket with your fare when you get off the bus. (If you get on at the terminal station, you don't get a ticket.)

EXPRESSIONS IN CONTEXT

Kanda made itte kudasai.	Please go to Kanda.
Ano kado made itte kudasai.	Please go to that corner.
Hidari e magatte kudasai.	Please turn to the left.
Toranku o akete kudasai.	Please open the trunk.
Sumimasen. Migi e magatte kudasai.	Excuse me. Please turn right.
Koko de tomete kudasai.	Please stop here.
Ikura dess ka?	How much is it?
Kono basu wa Ginza ni tomarimahss ka?	Does this bus stop at Ginza?

Hai, tomarimahss.	Yes, it does.
Iie.	No. (it doesn't)
Tsuitara, oshiete kudasai.	Please tell me when we get there.
Sumimasen. Kore, kuzushite kudasai.	Excuse me. Please break this.
Sen-en satsu, kuzushite kudasai.	Please break this 1,000-yen note.
Dōmo arigatō.	Thank you.

TAXIS

takushii	taxi
kōsaten	intersection
Ano kōsaten de hidari e magatte kudasai.	Please turn left at that intersection.
shingō	traffic light
aka-shingō	red light
ao-shingō	green light
Oroshite kudasai.	Please let me out.
ryōshū-sho	receipt
Ryōshū-sho, kudasai.	Please give me a receipt.

BUSES

basu-tei	bus stop
Basu-tei wa doko dess ka?	Where's a bus stop?
buzā	buzzer (to indicate you want to get off)
san-ban basu	bus # 3

OTHERS

fune	ship
ferii	ferry
yūran-sen	excursion boat

nori-ba   entrance to board; landing
kippu   ticket
Kippu wa ikura dess ka?   How much is the ticket?

CHAPTER 8
Telling Time

To tell time, combine the numbers introduced on page 38 (**ichi, ni, san**, etc.) with **ji** (hour) and **fun** (minute). Remember that a.m. is **gozen**, and p.m. is **gogo**. These words go before the time, as in **gozen jū-ji** (10:00 a.m). Note that in some cases, **fun** changes to **pun**.

WORDS & EXPRESSIONS

ichi-ji	1:00
Ichi-ji dess.	It's 1:00.
gozen	a.m.
gogo	p.m.
yo-ji	4:00
Gogo yo-ji dess.	It's 4:00 p.m.
ip-pun	one minute
ni-fun	two minutes
san-pun	three minutes
yon-pun	four minutes
go-fun	five minutes
rop-pun	six minutes
shichi-fun/nana-fun	seven minutes
hachi-fun/hap-pun	eight minutes
kyū-fun	nine minutes
jup-pun	ten minutes
Gozen go-ji jup-pun dess.	It's 5:10 a.m.
mae	before
go-ji jup-pun mae	10 minutes before 5:00
han	half (past)
Gogo roku-ji-han dess.	It's 6:30 p.m.

ima	now
nan-ji	what time
Ima nan-ji dess ka?	What time is it now?
nan-ji ni	what time
dekakemahss	go out; leave
Nan-ji ni dekakemahss ka?	What time shall we go out?
asa-gohan	breakfast
Asa-gohan wa nan-ji dess ka?	What time is breakfast?
ban-gohan	supper
eiga	movie
hajimarimahss	start
Eiga wa nan-ji ni hajimarimahss ka?	What time does the movie start?

TIME INFORMATION

Trains and planes operate on the 24-hour timetable. Thus, midnight is 00:00, 9 a.m. is 09:00, and 5 p.m. is 17:00. If this is confusing, confirm times using the regular 12-hour method, carefully enunciating **gozen** (a.m.) or **gogo** (p.m.).

All of Japan lies in a single time zone that is one hour behind Sydney, one hour ahead of Hong Kong, nine hours ahead of London, and fourteen hours ahead of New York. If you want to confirm the time in any major city, dial 0051. That number connects you with KDD, Japan's largest international telephone service. The operators speak English.

EXPRESSIONS IN CONTEXT

Ima nan-ji dess ka?	What time is it now?
Hachi-ji dess.	It's 8:00.
Ku-ji go-fun dess.	It's 9:05.
Jū-ji nana-fun mae dess.	It's 7 minutes before 10:00.
Ichi-ji san-jup-pun dess.	It's 1:30.
Ni-ji-han dess.	It's 2:30.

Gozen roku-ji ni-jū-go-fun dess.	It's 6:25 a.m.
Gogo yo-ji-han dess.	It's 4:30 p.m.
Ban-gohan wa nan-ji dess ka?	What time is supper?
Shichi-ji jū-go-fun dess.	It's at 7:15.
Eiga wa nan-ji dess ka?	What time is the movie?
San-ji yon-jū-go-fun dess.	It's at 3:45.
Nan-ji ni hajimarimahss ka?	What time does it start?
Go-ji ni-jup-pun dess.	At 5:20.
Kabuki wa nan-ji dess ka?	What time is the Kabuki performance?
Hachi-ji ni hajimarimahss.	It starts at 8:00.
Nan-ji ni dekakemahss ka?	What time shall we leave?
Shichi-ji-han ni dekakemahss.	We'll leave at 7:30.

ADDITIONAL WORDS & EXPRESSIONS

gohan	meal; cooked rice
hiru-gohan	lunch
o-cha no jikan	teatime
tōchaku-jikan	arrival time
shuppatsu-jikan	departure time
Shuppatsu-jikan wa nan-ji dess ka?	What time do we depart?
kaimaku-jikan	the time a performance starts
kaiten-jikan	opening hour of a store
heiten-jikan	closing hour of a store
shūgō-jikan	meeting time
kaisan-jikan	break-up time; the time a group disperses
yakusoku	promise; engagement; appointment
yakusoku no jikan	time set for an appointment
tokei	watch; clock
mezamashi-dokei	alarm clock
Mezamashi-dokei ga arimahss ka?	Do you have an alarm clock?

CHAPTER 9
Days of the Week

The key to improving your Japanese is to use it every chance you get. Don't be embarrassed and don't get discouraged. One tip: avoid putting stress in your speech. You're much better off speaking in a monotone than stressing the wrong syllables.

WORDS & EXPRESSIONS

kyō	today
Getsu-yōbi	Monday
Kyō wa Getsu-yōbi dess.	Today is Monday.
ashita	tomorrow
Ka-yōbi	Tuesday
Ashita wa Ka-yōbi dess.	Tomorrow is Tuesday.
Sui-yōbi	Wednesday
Moku-yōbi	Thursday
Kin-yōbi	Friday
Do-yōbi	Saturday
Nichi-yōbi	Sunday
kinō	yesterday
deshita	was; were
Kinō wa Nichi-yōbi deshita.	Yesterday was Sunday.
asatte	day after tomorrow
nan-yōbi	what day (of the week)
kankō	sightseeing
Kankō wa nan-yōbi dess ka?	What day is for sightseeing?
kekkon-shiki	wedding ceremony
hakuran-kai	exposition
pātii	party

Pātii wa nan-yōbi dess ka?	What day is the party?
Do-yōbi dess.	It's Saturday.
sōbetsu-kai	farewell party
pikunikku	picnic
kengaku-ryokō	field trip; tour of a factory, institution, etc.
yasumi	holiday; day off

MEANINGS OF THE DAYS OF THE WEEKS

In Japanese, the days of the week derive from the world of nature. **Getsu-yōbi** (Monday), means "moon day"; **Ka-yōbi** (Tuesday), "fire day"; **Sui-yōbi** (Wednesday), "water day"; **Moku-yōbi** (Thursday) "wood day"; **Kin-yōbi** (Friday), "gold day"; **Do-yōbi** (Saturday) "soil day"; and **Nichi-yōbi** (Sunday), "sun day." Interestingly enough, our Sunday and Monday derive from the sun and moon as well, but here the similarity stops.

EXPRESSIONS IN CONTEXT

Kyō wa nan-yōbi dess ka?	What day is today?
Getsu-yōbi dess.	It's Monday.
Ashita wa nan-yōbi dess ka?	What day is tomorrow?
Kin-yōbi dess.	It's Friday.
Kekkon-shiki wa nan-yōbi dess ka?	What day is the wedding ceremony?
Asatte dess.	The day after tomorrow.
Hakuran-kai wa nan-yōbi dess ka?	What day is the exposition?
Moku-yōbi dess.	Thursday.
Pikunikku wa Do-yōbi dess ka?	Is the picnic on Saturday?
Iie, Ka-yōbi dess.	No, it's on Tuesday.
Kinō wa nan-yōbi deshita ka?	What day was yesterday?
Nichi-yōbi deshita.	It was Sunday.

Sōbetsu-kai wa nan-yōbi deshita ka?	What day was the farewell party?
Getsu-yōbi deshita.	It was Monday.
Yasumi wa nan-yōbi deshita ka?	What day did you take off from work?
Ka-yōbi deshita.	I took off Tuesday.
Kengaku-ryokō wa Sui-yōbi deshita ka?	Was the field trip on Wednesday?
Iie, Kin-yōbi deshita.	No, it was on Friday.

DAYS AND WEEKS

ototoi	day before yesterday
mae no hi	previous day
tsugi no hi	next day
heijitsu	weekday
shūmatsu	weekend
saijitsu	national holiday
kyūka	day off from work
karendā	calendar
konshū	this week
raishū	next week
senshū	last week
sen-senshū	week before last

EVENTS

enkai	banquet
kakuteru-pātii	cocktail party
kangei-kai	welcome party
o-sōshiki	funeral
konsāto	concert
shiai	game; match
gorufu no konpe	golf tournament

yakyū no shiai   baseball game
hanabi   fireworks
hanabi-taikai   fireworks display

Yotei	
Shi-gatsu 23-29 nichi	
Nichi-yōbi	tenisu no shiai
Getsu-yōbi	Jēn no kekkonshiki
Ka-yōbi	M-sensei shinsatsu
Sui-yōbi	Jon to yakusoku
Moku-yōbi	eiga kanshō
Kin-yōbi	An to ranchi
Do-yōbi	Uchi de kyūsoku

CHAPTER 10

Days, Months, Years

Remembering the names of the months is simple in Japanese. Just combine numbers (see page 38) with **gatsu** (month). Thus, **Hachi-gatsu** is the eighth month, August; **Jū-ni-gatsu** is the twelfth month, December; and **Ichi-gatsu** is the first month, January.

WORDS & EXPRESSIONS

kyō	today
tsuitachi	the 1st
Kyō wa tsuitachi dess.	Today is the 1st.
ashita	tomorrow
Ashita wa futsuka dess.	Tomorrow is the 2nd.
mikka	the 3rd
yokka	the 4th
itsuka	the 5th
muika	the 6th
nanoka	the 7th
nan-nichi	what day (of the month)
Nan-nichi dess ka?	What's the date?
tenran-kai	exhibition
Tenran-kai wa nan-nichi dess ka?	What's the date of the exhibition?
o-matsuri	festival
kongetsu	this month
Ichi-gatsu	January
Kongetsu wa Ichi-gatsu dess.	This month is January.
raigetsu	next month
Ni-gatsu	February
Raigetsu wa Ni-gatsu dess.	Next month is February.

San-gatsu	March
Shi-gatsu	April
Go-gatsu	May
Roku-gatsu	June
Shichi-gatsu	July
Hachi-gatsu	August
Ku-gatsu	September
Jū-gatsu	October
Jū-ichi-gatsu	November
Jū-ni-gatsu	December
Nan-gatsu dess ka?	What month is it?
Nan-gatsu nan-nichi dess ka?	What month and what day is it?

THE MOON AND THE MONTHS

Gatsu (month), a variant of **getsu** as in **Getsu-yōbi** (Monday), literally means "moon." The moon, as we know, became associated with months because it completes one cycle in a four-week period. You could think of the Japanese months as first moon, second moon, third moon, and so on.

Speaking of the moon, the Japanese have long celebrated "moon viewing." Called **tsuki-mi**, it was often a gathering of nobles and courtiers who relaxed on a veranda, gazed at the autumn moon, and composed short, poetic verses.

EXPRESSIONS IN CONTEXT

Kyō wa nan-nichi dess ka?	What's the date today?
Itsuka dess.	It's the 5th.
Ashita wa nan-nichi dess ka?	What's the date tomorrow?
Muika dess.	It's the 6th.
O-matsuri wa nan-nichi dess ka?	What's the date of the festival?
Tsuitachi dess.	It's the 1st.

Kongetsu wa nan-gatsu dess ka?	What month is this month?
Ichi-gatsu dess.	It's January.
Tenran-kai wa nan-gatsu dess ka?	What month is the exhibition?
Ni-gatsu dess.	It's February.
Tenran-kai wa raigetsu dess.	The exhibition is next month.
Kyō wa nan-gatsu nan-nichi dess ka?	What's the date today?
Roku-gatsu tsuitachi dess.	It's June 1st.
Ku-gatsu nanoka dess.	It's September 7th.
Tenran-kai wa nan-gatsu nan-nichi dess ka?	What's the date of the exhibition?
Raigetsu futsuka dess.	The 2nd of next month.

DAYS OF THE MONTH

yōka	the 8th
kokonoka	the 9th
tōka	the 10th
jū-ichi-nichi	the 11th
jū-ni-nichi	the 12th
jū-san-nichi	the 13th
jū-yokka	the 14th
jū-go-nichi	the 15th
jū-roku-nichi	the 16th
jū-shichi-nichi	the 17th
jū-hachi-nichi	the 18th
jū-ku-nichi	the 19th
hatsuka	the 20th
ni-jū-ichi-nichi	the 21st
ni-jū-ni-nichi	the 22nd
ni-jū-san-nichi	the 23rd

ni-jū-yokka	the 24th
ni-jū-go-nichi	the 25th
ni-jū-roku-nichi	the 26th
ni-jū-shichi-nichi	the 27th
ni-jū-hachi-nichi	the 28th
ni-jū-ku-nichi	the 29th
san-jū-nichi	the 30th
san-jū-ichi-nichi	the 31st

YEARS

kotoshi	this year
kyonen	last year
ototoshi	year before last
rainen	next year
sarainen	year after next
mai-nen/mai-toshi	every year
sen-kyū-hyaku kyū-jū-nen	1990
nan-nen	what year
Kotoshi wa nan-nen dess ka?	What year is this year?
Sen-kyū-hyaku kyū-jū-ichi-nen dess.	It's 1991.

OTHERS

kisetsu	season
haru	spring
natsu	summer
aki	autumn
fuyu	winter
mai-nichi	everyday
mai-ban	every night

sengetsu	last month
mai-tsuki/mai-getsu	every month
tanjō-bi	birthday
kinen-bi	anniversary

CHAPTER 11
Asking About Times

Need to know when something will take place? For time, say **Nan-ji dess ka?** (What time is it/ will it be?) and for dates, **Itsu dess ka?** (When is it?) When asking a stranger a question, remember to start off with **Sumimasen**. (For information about numbers, see Chapter 5.)

WORDS & EXPRESSIONS

itsu	when
Kabuki wa itsu dess ka?	When is the Kabuki performance?
konban	tonight; this evening
Konban dess.	It's tonight.
shinai-kankō	tour of a city
nan-ji	what time
Shinai-kankō wa nan-ji dess ka?	What time is the city tour?
asa-gohan	breakfast
~ no ato (de)	after ~
Asa-gohan no ato dess.	It's after breakfast.
Kyūshū-meguri	tour of Kyushu
-meguri	tour of
ashita	tomorrow
Kyūshū-meguri wa ashita dess ka?	Is the Kyushu tour tomorrow?
Hai. Sō dess.	Yes, it is.
onsen	hot spring
onsen e	to a hot spring
Itsu onsen e ikimahss ka?	When will you go to the hot spring?
Konshū ikimahss.	I'll go this week.
hakubutsu-kan	museum

nan-yōbi	what day of the week
nan-yōbi ni	on what day of the week
Nan-yōbi ni hakubutsu-kan e ikimahss ka?	On what day will you go to the museum?
Do-yōbi ni	on Saturday
Do-yōbi ni ikimahss.	I'll go on Saturday.
ku-ji ni	at 9:00
Ku-ji ni ikimahss.	I'll go at 9:00.
tōka ni	on the 10th
Tōka ni ikimahss.	I'll go on the 10th.

NI, E, AND WA

Here's some advice on how to use three important particles: **ni, e,** and **wa**. Use **ni** as you would "at" or "on" in a time-related expression like "*at* 9:30" (**ku-ji-han ni**) or "I go *on* the 10th" (**Tōka ni ikimahss**). For **e**, think of "to" when it refers to destinations, as in "I go *to* Tokyo" (**Tōkyō e ikimahss**). **Wa** has no corresponding English equivalent. In general, **wa** comes after the subject of a sentence, as in **Watashi wa Amerika-jin dess** (I'm American) or **Hoteru wa ii dess** (The hotel is nice). For now, whenever you say **watashi** (I), follow it with **wa**.

EXPRESSIONS IN CONTEXT

Itsu dess ka?	When is it?
Tōka dess.	It's on the 10th.
Do-yōbi dess.	It's on Saturday.
Shinai-kankō wa Getsu-yōbi dess ka?	Is the city tour on Monday?
Nan-ji dess ka?	What time will it be?
Asa-gohan no ato dess.	It's after breakfast.
Kyūshū-meguri wa itsu dess ka?	When is the Kyushu tour?
Konshū dess.	It's this week.

Tōka dess.	It's on the 10th.
Itsu onsen e ikimahss ka?	When will you go to the hot spring?
Konshū ikimahss.	I'll go this week.
Itsu hakubutsu-kan e ikimahss ka?	When will you go to the museum?
Asa-gohan no ato de ikimahss.	I'll go after breakfast.
Jū-ji ni ikimahss.	I'll go at 10:00.
Nan-yōbi ni ikimahss ka?	On what day will you go?
Konban ikimahss ka?	Will you go tonight?

SCHEDULING

shokuji	meal
no mae (ni)	before
shokuji no mae	before a meal
ashita no asa	tomorrow morning
sugu	right away
mō sugu	soon; shortly
chikai uchi ni	one of these days
Chikai uchi ni ikimahss.	I'll go one of these days.
mai-shū	every week
raishū	next week
senshū	last week
natsu-yasumi	summer vacation
fuyu-yasumi	winter vacation
ryokō-sha	traveler
ryokō-sentā	travel bureau
dantai-ryokō	group tour
Dantai-ryokō de ikimahss.	I'll go with a group tour.
hitori	alone
Hitori de ikimahss.	I'll go by myself.

kaigai-ryokō overseas travel
ryokō-hoken travel insurance
gaido-bukku guidebook

CHAPTER 12
Talking About Food

If you plan to have a meal with Japanese people, you should master two phrases: **itadakimahss and gochisō-sama deshita**. Say **itadakimahss** before you start eating and **gochisō-sama deshita** when you have finished. All Japanese say these phrases at meals, and you'll leave a good impression if you do too.

WORDS & EXPRESSIONS

o-cha	green tea
o	(direct object particle)
dōzo	please (do something)
O-cha o dōzo.	Please have some tea.
Itadakimahss.	Thank you. (I'll have some.)
Kekkō dess.	No, thank you.
o-kashi	sweets
ikaga	how about
O-kashi wa ikaga dess ka?	How about some sweets?
kore	this
nan(i)	what
Kore wa nan dess ka?	What's this?
o-manjū	(bun with bean-jam filling)
O-manjū dess.	It's a **manjū**.
naka	inside
Naka wa nan dess ka?	What's inside?
donna	what kind of
aji	taste
Donna aji dess ka?	What does it taste like?
amai	sweet

oishii	delicious
ne?	isn't it?
Oishii dess ne?	It's delicious, isn't it?
Gochisō-sama deshita.	Thank you. (It was delicious.)
motto	more; some more
Motto ikaga dess ka?	How about some more?
o-naka	stomach
ga	(subject particle)
suite imahss	hungry
O-naka ga suite imahss.	I'm hungry.
ippai	full
O-naka ga ippai dess.	I'm full.
kukkii	cookie

LOANWORDS

Thousands of words in Japanese are loanwords, words derived from other languages. Try guessing the meanings of these drinks: **Koka-kōra, kōhii,** and **biiru**. Did you guess Coca-Cola, coffee, and beer? With exposure, you can easily increase your vocabulary just by learning loanwords.

Be careful, though, because not all loanwords come from English. For instance, **pan** (bread) comes from Portuguese, **ikura** (salmon roe) from Russian, and **arubaito** (part-time job) from German.

EXPRESSIONS IN CONTEXT

O-kashi o dōzo.	Please have some sweets.
Hai, itadakimahss.	Thank you.
Iie, kekkō dess.	No, thank you.
Kore wa nan dess ka?	What's this?
Naka wa nan dess ka?	What's inside?

Donna aji dess ka?	What does it taste like?
O-manjū wa ikaga dess ka?	How about a manjū?
Hai, itadakimahss.	Thank you.
Oishii dess ne?	Delicious, isn't it?
Amai dess ne?	Sweet, isn't it?
O-kashi wa oishii dess ne?	The sweets are delicious, aren't they?
Motto ikaga dess ka?	How about some more?
Iie, kekkō dess.	No, thank you.
O-naka ga ippai dess.	I'm full.
Gochisō-sama deshita.	Thank you. (It was wonderful.)
O-naka ga suite imahss.	I'm hungry.
Kukkii o dōzo.	Please have some cookies.
Itadakimahss.	Thank you. (I'll have some.)

DESCRIBING FOOD

nama	raw
mazui	not tasty
atarashii	new; fresh
furui	old; stale
katai	hard; tough
yawarakai	soft; tender
atsui	hot
tsumetai	cold (to the touch)
karai	spicy
shoppai	salty
suppai	sour
nigai	bitter

DRINKS

mizu	water
kōhii	coffee
kōcha	black tea
biiru	beer
wain	wine
Koka-kōra	Coca-Cola
shōchū	(distilled spirit usually drunk with water or a mixer)
uisukii	whiskey
mizu-wari	whiskey and water

FRUIT

kuda-mono; furūtsu	fruit
ringo	apple
nashi	pear
momo	peach
budō	grape
mikan	tangerine
orenji	orange
suika	watermelon
meron	melon
kaki	persimmon

VEGETABLES

yasai	vegetable
retasu	lettuce
kyabetsu	cabbage
kabocha	pumpkin

tomato	tomato
jagaimo	potato
kyūri	cucumber
tōmorokoshi	corn
tamanegi	onion
nasu	eggplant
ninjin	carrot
shiitake	type of mushroom
renkon	lotus root
takenoko	bamboo shoot
sarada	salad

MEAT, SEAFOOD, POULTRY, DAIRY PRODUCTS

niku	meat
gyū-niku	beef
buta-niku	pork
sakana	fish
ebi	shrimp
ika	cuttlefish
tako	octopus
gyū-nyū	milk
yōguruto	yogurt
aisu-kuriimu	ice cream
tori-niku	chicken
tamago	egg

OTHERS

gohan	cooked rice (can also mean "meal")
raisu	rice (usually rice served with non-Japanese dishes)

tōfu	tofu
miso	miso (bean paste)
nori	seaweed
o-hashi	chopsticks
kēki	cake
senbei	rice cracker
Kore wa dō-yatte tabemahss ka?	How do you eat this?
nan de	with what
Kore wa nan de tabemahss ka?	What do you eat this with?

CHAPTER 13

Dining Out

Travelers should not miss eating at a restaurant where the local residents are the main patrons. (Your hotel should know a good one nearby.) If you don't know what to order, try a set meal called a **teishoku**. Ask **Teishoku ga arimahss ka?** (Do you have set meals?) to find out if the restaurant serves them or not.

WORDS & EXPRESSIONS

kono	this
hen	vicinity
kono hen ni	in this vicinity; around here
resutoran	restaurant
ga	(subject particle)
arimahss	there is; there are
Kono hen ni resutoran ga arimahss ka?	Is there a restaurant around here?
tenpura	tempura (deep-fried food)
wa	(subject particle, frequently used in negative sentences)
arimasen	don't have
Tenpura wa arimasen.	We don't have tempura.
nani	what
Nani ga arimahss ka?	What do you have?
o-nomimono	drink
O-nomimono wa?	How about a drink?
biiru	beer
o-negai shimahss	please (*lit.,* I make a request)
Biiru, o-negai shimahss.	Beer, please.
o-sake	saké (Japanese rice wine)

o-sushi	sushi (vinegared rice and raw fish)
kudasai	please give
O-sushi, kudasai.	Sushi, please.
Sumimasen.	Excuse me.
mizu	water
Sumimasen. Mizu, kudasai.	Excuse me. May I have some water?
karē-raisu	curry with rice
Karē-raisu, kudasai.	Curry with rice, please.
Kashikomarimashita.	Certainly, sir/ma'am.

EATING IN JAPANESE RESTAURANTS

Eating in Japan is a great experience. The food is good, healthy, and there's a great variety to choose from. But what if you can't read the menu? There's no need to worry, because many places have plastic food displays. Just take the waiter to the display case, and point to what you want to eat.

One tip for sushi lovers. If you don't know how to order sushi, call out **Nigiri-zushi, ichinin-mae!** and you'll get a tray of various types of sushi. You can also point, this time to the real thing, to other delicacies you want to try.

EXPRESSIONS IN CONTEXT

Kono hen ni resutoran ga arimahss ka?	Is there a restaurant around here?
Hai, arimahss.	Yes, there is.
Iie, arimasen.	No, there isn't.
Tenpura ga arimahss ka?	Do you have tempura?
Hai, arimahss.	Yes, we have.
Tenpura, o-negai shimahss.	Tempura, please.
Kashikomarimashita.	Certainly, sir.
Karē-raisu ga arimahss ka?	Do you have curry with rice?
Iie, karē-raisu wa arimasen.	No, we don't have curry with rice.

Nani ga arimahss ka?	What do you have?
Karē raisu ga arimahss.	We have curry with rice.
O-sushi ga arimahss ka?	Do you have sushi?
Iie, o-sushi wa arimasen.	No, we don't have sushi.
O-nomimono wa?	How about a drink?
O-sake, kudasai.	Saké, please.
Mizu, o-negai shimahss.	Water, please.
Sumimasen. Biiru, kudasai.	Excuse me. Beer, please.

MENU ITEMS

Nihon-ryōri	Japanese cuisine
Chūgoku-ryōri	Chinese cuisine
Seiyō-ryōri	Western cuisine
teishoku	set meal (includes main dish, soup, pickles, and rice)
gohan	rice
sui-mono	soup
tsuke-mono	pickle
suki-yaki	popular dish of meat, vegetable, bean curd, etc.
yaki-tori	grilled, skewered chicken
ton-katsu	pork cutlet
una-don	broiled eel and rice
udon	noodles (white and fat)
soba	buckwheat noodles (dark and thin)

TABLEWARE

chawan	rice bowl
yu-nomi	teacup

koppu	cup; glass
tokkuri	saké bottle
sakazuki	saké cup
sara	plate
o-hashi	chopsticks
o-shibori	hot or cold hand towel used to wipe one's hands before eating
fōku	fork
supūn	spoon
napukin	napkin

OTHERS

Kore wa dō-yatte tabemahss ka?	How do you eat this?
nan de	with what
Kore wa nan de tabemahss ka?	With what do you eat this?
o-kanjō	check
O-kanjō, o-negai shimahss.	May I please have the check?
Betsu-betsu ni, o-negai shimahss.	We'd like to pay separately.
Ikura dess ka?	How much is it?
kurejitto-kādo	credit card
Kurejitto-kādo de haraemahss ka?	May I pay with a credit card?
Oishii dess.	It's delicious.
Oishikatta dess.	It was delicious.

CHAPTER 14
Making Telephone Calls

To use a public phone, put in a ten-yen coin, wait for a dial tone, and dial. If you're calling within your area code, you can speak three minutes for ten yen; the same amount will give you less time for calls outside your area code. Insert more if you need to talk longer. You'll receive your unused coins when you hang up.

WORDS & EXPRESSIONS

Moshi-moshi.	Hello. (on the telephone)
o-negai shimahss	please
Yamada-san, o-negai shimahss.	Mr. Yamada, please. (May I speak with Mr. Yamada?)
shibaraku	a moment; awhile
o-machi kudasai	please wait
Shibaraku o-machi kudasai.	Please wait a moment.
Konnichiwa.	Hello./Good afternoon.
O-genki dess ka?	How are you?
Sumimasen ga...	Sorry, but...
ima	now
imasen	isn't in; aren't in
Sumimasen ga, Yamada wa ima imasen.	Sorry, but Mr. Yamada isn't in now.
dochira-sama	who
Dochira-sama dess ka?	Who is calling, please?
O-namae wa?	What's your name?
yoku	well
kikoemasen	can't hear
Yoku kikoemasen.	I can't hear well.
mō ichido	once more
itte kudasai	please say

Mō ichido itte kudasai.	Please say it once more.
Ei-go	English language
Ei-go de	in English
Ei-go de itte kudasai.	Please say it in English.
mata	again
o-denwa	telephone
o-denwa shimahss	make a telephone call
Mata o-denwa shimahss.	I'll call again.
Sayōnara.	Goodbye.

TELEPHONES

The three most common types of public phones are red, yellow, and green phones. Red phones take only 10-yen coins, yellow telephones take 10-yen and 100-yen coins, and green telephones take telephone cards and usually 10-yen and 100-yen coins. Telephone cards come in denominations of 500 yen, 1,000 yen, and higher, and can be used instead of coins. You can purchase these telephone cards, available in a huge assortment of designs, at newsstands, vending machines, telephone offices, and convenience stores.

For helpful telephone services in English, refer to page 109.

EXPRESSIONS IN CONTEXT

Moshi-moshi. Yamada-san, o-negai shimahss?	Hello. May I speak to Mr. Yamada?
Hai. Shibaraku o-machi kudasai.	Yes. Please wait a moment.
Moshi-moshi. Yamada dess.	Hello. Yamada speaking.
Konnichiwa, Yamada san. Buraun dess.	Hello, Mr. Yamada. This is Brown speaking.
Konnichiwa, Buraun-san. O-genki dess ka?	Hello, Mr. Brown. How are you?
Hai, arigatō. Genki dess.	Yes, I'm fine, thank you.

Sumimasen ga, yoku kikoemasen.	Excuse me, but I can't hear well.
Ei-go de mō ichido itte kudasai.	Please say it once more in English.
Moshi-moshi. Yamada-san wa imahss ka?	Hello. Is Mr. Yamada in?
Sumimasen ga, Yamada wa ima imasen.	Sorry, but he isn't in now.
Dochira-sama dess ka?	Who is calling, please?
Buraun dess. Mata o-denwa shimahss.	This is Brown. I'll call again.
Hai, o-negai shimahss.	Yes, please do.
Sayōnara.	Goodbye.

ADDITIONAL WORDS & EXPRESSIONS

denwa-bangō	telephone number
denwa-chō	telephone directory
keitai-denwa	cell phone
denwa-ryō	telephone bill
kōshū-denwa	public telephone
shinai-denwa	local telephone call
chōkyori-denwa	long distance telephone call
kokusai-denwa	international telephone call
kōkan-shu	operator
korekuto-kōru	collect call
kurejitto-kādo	credit card
terefon-kādo	telephone card
messēji	message
Messēji wa o-negai dekimahss ka?	May I leave a message?
naisen	extension
bangō-chigai	wrong number
Bangō ga chigaimahss.	You have the wrong number.
O-denwa o karite mo ii dess ka?	May I use this phone?
O-denwa, dōmo arigatō.	Thank you for calling.
O-denwa wa doko dess ka?	Where's a phone?

CHAPTER 15
Describing Your Plans

When you speak Japanese, use short, easy phrases. Try to simplify your language; for example, rather than trying to say "I intend to spend time looking at old Japanese Buddhist temples," say "I'll see temples." That becomes simply **O-tera o mimahss**.

WORDS & EXPRESSIONS

ashita	tomorrow
Kyōto	Kyoto
Kyōto e	to Kyoto
ikimahss	go
Ashita Kyōto e ikimahss.	Tomorrow I'll go to Kyoto.
Kyōto de	in Kyoto; at Kyoto
nani	what
o	(object particle)
shimahss	do
Kyōto de nani o shimahss ka?	What will you do in Kyoto?
o-tera	Buddhist temple
mimahss	see
O-tera o mimahss.	I'll see temples.
yūmei na	famous
Yūmei na o-tera e ikimahss.	I'll go to a famous temple.
niwa	garden
Yūmei na niwa o mimahss.	I'll see famous gardens.
shashin	photo
torimahss	take
Shashin o torimahss.	I'll take some photos.
Kyōto de shashin o torimahss.	I'll take photos in Kyoto.

e-hagaki	postcard
kaimahss	buy
E-hagaki o kaimahss.	I'll buy some postcards.
O-tera de e-hagaki o kaimahss.	I'll buy some postcards at the temple.
o-miyage	souvenir
kōen	park
kōen made	to the park
arukimahss	walk
Kōen made arukimahss.	I'll walk to the park.

ENCHANTING KYOTO

Every visitor to Japan should experience wandering around Kyoto's back streets. Wherever you turn, you'll discover a myriad of shrines, temples, and traditional shops and residences. And in these back streets, you'll also find a peace and quiet that is rare in most other cities.

Because of its vast number of cultural treasures (there are over 400 shrines and 1,600 temples alone), Kyoto was not bombed in World War II. Thus, Kyoto remains Japan's cultural capital, a proud city that gave rise to one of the world's most refined civilizations.

EXPRESSIONS IN CONTEXT

Ashita Tōkyō e ikimahss.	I'll go to Tokyo tomorrow.
Ashita kōen e ikimahss.	I'll go to the park tomorrow.
Ashita yūmei na niwa e ikimahss.	I'll go to a famous garden tomorrow.
Kyōto de nani o mimahss ka?	What will you see in Kyoto?
Yūmei na niwa o mimahss.	I'll see famous gardens.
Nani o shimahss ka?	What will you do?
Kōen made arukimahss.	I'll walk to the park.
Kōen de shashin o torimahss.	I'll take some photographs in the park.

Nani o mimahss ka?	What will you see?
Yūmei na kōen o mimahss.	I'll see a famous park.
Kyōto de shashin o torimahss ka?	Will you take some photos in Kyoto?
Hai, torimahss.	Yes, I will.
Nani o kaimahss ka?	What will you buy?
O-miyage o kaimahss.	I'll buy some souvenirs.

SPARE-TIME ACTIVITIES

zasshi	magazine
hon	book
shinbun	newspaper
Zasshi o yomimahss.	I'll read a magazine.
terebi	television
rajio	radio
Rajio o kikimahss.	I'll listen to the radio.
tegami	letter
Tegami o kakimahss.	I'll write a letter.
hoteru e	to the hotel
Hoteru e kaerimahass.	I'll return to the hotel.
orenji-jūsu	orange juice
Orenji-jūsu o nomimahss.	I'll drink orange juice.
hayaku	early
Hayaku okimahss.	I'll get up early.
osoku	late
Osoku nemahss.	I'll go to bed late.

CHAPTER 16
Describing What You Did

If a Japanese word ends in **mashita**, you can be almost certain that it is a verb in its past tense. For example, the present tense of the verb "to go" is **ikimahss** and the past tense is **ikimashita**. The present tense of the verb "to do" is **shimahss** and the past tense is **shimashita**. There are few exceptions to this rule.

WORDS & EXPRESSIONS

kinō	yesterday
doko	where
e	to
doko e	where to
ikimashita	went
Kinō doko e ikimashita ka?	Where did you go yesterday?
Nara	Nara
Nara e	to Nara
Nara e ikimashita.	I went to Nara.
Nara de	in Nara
nani	what
o	(object particle)
shimashita	did
Nara de nani o shimashita ka?	What did you do in Nara?
daibutsu	large statue of Buddha
mimashita	saw
Nara de daibutsu o mimashita.	I saw the large statue of Buddha in Nara.
kōen	park
arukimashita	walked
Kōen made arukimashita.	I walked to the park.

shashin	photograph
torimashita	took
Shashin o torimashita.	I took some photos.
shika	deer (Nara is famous for its deer.)
no	of
shika no shashin	photo of deer
o-miyage	souvenir
kaimashita	bought
O-miyage o kaimashita.	I bought souvenirs.

ORIGIN OF THE JAPANESE LANGUAGE

Where did the Japanese spoken language come from? No one knows for sure. Some feel there's a strong connection with the Altaic languages of Central Asia. Others believe Japanese derived from the languages of Southeast Asia and Polynesia. And a few insist that Japanese has no connections at all with any other language.

The writing system, on the other hand, came from China in the sixth century. At that time, Buddhism was being introduced from China, and a writing system was necessary to propagate the wisdom of the sutras.

EXPRESSIONS IN CONTEXT

Doko e ikimashita ka?	Where did you go?
Kyōto e ikimashita.	I went to Kyoto.
O-tera e ikimashita.	I went to a Buddhist temple.
Kōen e ikimashita.	I went to the park.
Nara de nani o mimashita ka?	What did you see in Nara?
O-tera o mimashita.	I saw Buddhist temples.
Kōen o mimashita.	I saw the park.
Shika o mimashita.	I saw deer.
Nani o shimashita ka?	What did you do?

Shashin o torimashita.	I took some photos.
Nani o mimashita ka?	What did you see?
O-tera o mimashita ka?	Did you see Buddhist temples?
Shashin o torimashita ka?	Did you take photos?
Hai, torimashita. Shika no shashin o torimashita.	Yes, I did. I took photos of the deer.
Nani o kaimashita ka?	What did you buy?
O-miyage o kaimashita.	I bought some souvenirs.

ADDITIONAL WORDS & EXPRESSIONS

daigaku	college; university
tosho-kan	library
eiga-kan	movie theater
gekijō	theater
garō	gallery
sutajiamu	stadium
hiro-ba	public square
shiseki	historical site
Shiseki e ikimashita.	I went to a historical site.
kinen-hi	monument
zō	statue
meisho	place of interest (tourist spots)
Kono hen ni meisho wa arimahss ka?	Are there any tourists spots around here?
meisan	regional specialty
Kono hen no meisan wa nan dess ka?	What product is this area famous for?
nyūjō-ken	admission ticket
Nyūjō-ken o kaimashita.	I bought an admission ticket.
nyūjō-ryō	admission fee
Nyūjō-ryō wa ikura dess ka?	How much is the admission fee?

CHAPTER 17

Expressing What You Want

Remember that communicating is your objective. Don't worry if your particles are wrong or your word order is incorrect. If you're unsure about a particle, simply skip over it. The truth is that many Japanese drop particles in conversation, so it's not a problem if you do too.

WORDS & EXPRESSIONS

Nihon ningyō	Japanese doll
ga	(subject particle)
hoshii	want
Nihon ningyō ga hoshii dess.	I want a Japanese doll.
ryokan	Japanese inn
suki	like
Ryokan ga suki dess.	I like Japanese inns.
hoteru	hotel
wa	(subject particle, frequently used in negative sentences)
suki dewa arimasen	don't like
Hoteru wa suki dewa arimasen.	I don't like hotels.
nani	what
o	(direct object particle)
shi-tai	want to do
Nani o shi-tai dess ka?	What do you want to do?
sumō	traditional Japanese wrestling
mi-tai	want to see
Sumō o mi-tai dess.	I want to see sumo.
Fuji-san e	to Mount Fuji

iki-tai	want to go
Fuji-san e iki-tai dess.	I want to go to Mount Fuji.
hanga	woodblock print
kai-tai	want to buy
Hanga o kai-tai dess.	I want to buy woodblock prints.
seto-mono	pottery
yukkuri	slowly
hanashite kudasai	please speak
Yukkuri hanashite kudasai.	Please speak slowly.
shashin	photograph
totte kudasai	please take
Shashin o totte kudasai.	Please take a picture.

MOUNT FUJI

Japan's most revered mountain, Mount Fuji, is called **Fuji-san** in Japanese. **San**, which here means "mountain" and not "Mr.", is used with other Japanese mountains like Asosan in Kyushu and Hiei-zan in Kyoto.

At 12,385 feet, Mount Fuji is Japan's highest mountain, and although it last erupted in 1707, it's classified as an active volcano. From the bullet train, you can get a good view of Mount Fuji's superb conical shape. The adventurous can climb it; people of all ages climb Mount Fuji, mostly to see the breathtaking sunrise over the Pacific Ocean.

EXPRESSIONS IN CONTEXT

Hanga ga hoshii dess.	I want a woodblock print.
Sumō ga suki dess.	I like sumo.
Hanga wa suki dewa arimasen.	I don't like woodblock prints.
Nani o shi-tai dess ka?	What do you want to do?
Kyōto e iki-tai dess.	I want to go to Kyoto.
Seto-mono o kai-tai dess.	I want to buy some pottery.

Nani o mi-tai dess ka?	What do you want to see?
Fuji-san o mi-tai dess.	I want to see Mount Fuji.
Sumō o mi-tai dess.	I want to see sumo.
Nani o kai-tai dess ka?	What do you want to buy?
Nihon ningyō o kai-tai dess.	I want to buy a Japanese doll.
Sumimasen. Yukkuri hanashite kudasai.	Excuse me. Please speak slowly.
Sumimasen. Shashin to totte kudasai.	Excuse me. Please take my picture.

ADDITIONAL WORDS & EXPRESSIONS

supōtsu	sports
undō	physical exercise
Undō o shi-tai dess.	I'd like to exercise.
umi	ocean
mizuumi	lake
yama	mountain
yama-nobori	mountain climbing
haikingu	hiking
kyanpu	camping
Kyanpu o shi-tai dess.	I want to go camping.
go	board game played with black and white stones
mājan	mahjong
e	painting
chōkoku	sculpture
kottō-hin	antique
Kottō-hin o mi-tai dess.	I want to see some antiques.
Sumimasen. Shashin o totte ii dess ka?	Excuse me. May I take a picture?
Anata no shashin o totte ii dess ka?	May I take your picture?

CHAPTER 18
Shopping

Shop clerks in Japan are polite and eager to help, and if you speak slowly and gesture, you shouldn't have problems making them understand you. Of course, understanding what **they** are saying is a different story. If you're unsure of a price, have a clerk write it down.

WORDS & EXPRESSIONS

ikura	how much
Ikura dess ka?	How much is it?
kore	this
Kore wa ikura dess ka?	How much is this?
ni-sen-en	2,000 yen
Ni-sen-en dess.	It's 2,000 yen.
ichi-man-en	10,000 yen
kono tokei	this watch
yon-man san-zen-en	43,000 yen
Kono tokei wa yon-man san-zen-en dess.	This watch is 43,000 yen.
o	(direct object particle)
kudasai	please; please give
Kore o kudasai.	Please give me this. (I'll take this.)
ōkii	big
ōkii-no	big one
misete kudasai	please show
Ōkii-no o misete kudasai.	Please show me a big one.
yasui	inexpensive
yasui-no	inexpensive one
Yasui-no o misete kudasai.	Please show me an inexpensive one.

hoka-no	different one
mō ichido	once more
itte kudasai	please say
Mō ichido itte kudasai.	Please say it once more.
Ei-go de	in English
hanashite kudasai	please speak
Ei-go de hanashite kudasai.	Please speak in English.
Nihon-go de	in Japanese
nedan	price
kaite kudasai	please write
Nedan o kaite kudasai.	Please write down the price.

FOLK-ART HANDICRAFTS

Mingei-hin, colorful folk-art handicrafts, make perfect gifts or souvenirs from Japan. As you travel, keep an eye out for local specialties. Tokyo, for example, is famous for its glass wind chimes (**fūrin**), Kyoto for its folding paper fans (**sensu**), and Tohoku for its delicately hand-painted wooden dolls (**kokeshi**). In most cities, **mingei-hin** are sold at small shops around tourist attractions and train stations. **Mingei** stores in larger cities have wonderful selections and fair prices, but they're often hard to find. It's a good idea to ask for directions.

EXPRESSIONS IN CONTEXT

Kore wa ikura dess ka?	How much is this?
Ni-sen-en dess.	It's 2,000 yen.
Ōkii-no wa ikura dess ka?	How much is the big one?
San-zen-en dess.	It's 3,000 yen.
Kono tokei wa ikura dess ka?	How much is this watch?
Yon-man-en dess.	It's 40,000 yen.
Ichi-man-en dess.	It's 10,000 yen.

Kore o kudasai.	Please give me this. (I'll take this.)
Kono tokei o kudasai.	Please give me this watch.
Kono yasui-no o kudasai.	Please give me this inexpensive one.
Kore o misete kudasai.	Please show me this.
Hoka-no o misete kudasai.	Please show me a different one.
Mō ichido misete kudasai.	Please show me once more.
Mō ichido itte kudasai.	Please say it once more.
Nihon-go de hanashite kudasai.	Please speak in Japanese.
Kore o kaite kudasai.	Please write this.

USEFUL ADJECTIVES

chiisai	small
takai	expensive
karui	light
omoi	heavy
marui	round
shikakui	square
azayaka	bright
jimi	subdued; refined
hade	flashy; gaudy
utsukushii	beautiful
kirei	pretty
furui	old
atarashii	new
dentō-teki	traditional

JAPANESE PRODUCTS

kinu	silk
ori-mono	cloth; textile

denki-seihin	electrical goods
nuri-mono	lacquerware
seto-mono	pottery
shippō-yaki	cloisonné ware
Imari-yaki	Imari ware
shinju	pearl
sensu	folding fan
mingei-hin	folk-art handicraft
furoshiki	cloth used for wrapping things
tōjiki	chinaware
kake-mono	hanging scroll; hanging picture
kimono	kimono
yukata	light, cotton kimono
chōchin	lantern
washi	traditional, handmade paper
hanga	woodblock print

OTHERS

chotto	a little; a moment
matte kudasai	please wait
Chotto matte kudasai.	Please wait a moment.
okutte kudasai	please send
Kore o okutte kudasai.	Please send this.
tsutsunde kudasai	please wrap
Kore o tsutsunde kudasai.	Please wrap this.

CHAPTER 19
Talking About the Weather

The Japanese believe they discuss the weather more than other people do. True or not, the weather offers you a good way to start a conversation. One thing is certain; the Japanese will be curious to know what type of weather you have in your part of the world.

WORDS & EXPRESSIONS

kyō	today
ii	good; nice
tenki	weather
ne	isn't it?
Kyō wa ii tenki dess ne?	It's nice weather today, isn't it?
Sō dess ne.	It is, isn't it?/That's right.
ashita	tomorrow
dō	how
deshō	will be; will probably be
Ashita wa dō deshō ka?	How will the weather be tomorrow?
shūmatsu	weekend
sā	well
ame	rain; rainy
Sā, ame deshō.	Well, it'll probably be rainy.
samui	cold (temperature)
Samui deshō.	It'll probably be cold.
kinō	yesterday
warui tenki	bad weather
deshita	was
Kinō wa warui tenki deshita.	The weather was bad yesterday.

atsui hi	hot day
Atsui hi deshita.	It was a hot day.
Hiroshima	Hiroshima
hare	fine weather
Hiroshima wa hare deshita.	The weather was fine in Hiroshima.
atatakai	warm
Kyō wa atatakai dess ne?	Today is warm, isn't it?
suzushii	cool

JAPANESE SEASONS

Japan has four major seasons—spring, summer, fall, and winter—with rainy periods between spring and summer, and summer and fall. During the fall rainy period, typhoons bring torrential rainfalls to all the country except Hokkai-do. Although the part of Japan bordering the Pacific Ocean has little snow in winter, areas like Kanazawa along the Japan Sea have heavy snowfalls that isolate rural villages. The change in landscape is dramatic. From Kyoto, which may have no snow on the grond, a train ride through a series of tunnels will take you to the heart of snow country in a matter of minutes.

EXPRESSIONS IN CONTEXT

Kyō wa ii tenki dess ne?	It's nice weather today, isn't it?
Sō dess ne.	It certainly is.
Suzushii dess ne?	Cool, isn't it?
Atsui dess ne?	Hot, isn't it?
Shūmatsu wa dō deshō ka?	How will it be this weekend?
Sā, hare deshō.	Well, it'll probably be fair.
Sā, ii tenki deshō.	Well, it'll probably be nice.
Kinō wa dō deshita ka?	How was yesterday?
Warui tenki deshita.	The weather was bad.

Ame deshita.	It was rainy.
Samui hi deshita.	It was a cold day.
Hiroshima wa dō deshita ka?	How was Hiroshima?
Hare deshita.	The weather was fine.
Ii tenki deshita.	The weather was nice.
Kinō wa warui tenki deshita ka?	Was the weather bad yesterday?
Iie, hare deshita.	No, it was fine.
Atatakai hi deshita.	It was a warm day.

ADDITIONAL WORDS & EXPRESSIONS

kikō	climate
tenki-yohō	weather forecast
Tenki-yohō ni yoru to, ashita wa ame dess.	According to the weather forecast, tomorrow will be rainy.
kishō-dai	weather bureau
ondo	temperature
Kashi	Fahrenheit
do	degree
Kashi nana-jū-do	70 degrees Fahrenheit
Sesshi	Celsius
Sesshi ni-jū-do	20 degrees Celsius
yuki	snow
furimahss	falls (rain, snow)
Ame ga furimahss.	It rains.
kiri	fog
sumoggu	smog
niwaka-ame	shower
kaze	wind
arashi	storm

taifū	typhoon
kaminari	thunder
inazuma	lightning
kumori	cloudy
mushi-atsui	humid
kasa	umbrella

CHAPTER 20
Making Reservations

Since making reservations on the phone in Japanese can be very difficult for the foreigner, it's fortunate that many places in Japan employ English-speaking staff to take reservations. Making reservations in person, however, is easier than on the phone. This chapter will teach you what to say.

WORDS & EXPRESSIONS

kankō-basu	tour bus
yoyaku	reservation
o-negai shimahss	please
Kankō-basu no yoyaku, o-negai shimahss.	I'd like to make a reservation for the tour bus.
Itsu dess ka?	For when?
Ashita dess.	For tomorrow.
kyō	today
man'in	full; no vacancy
Sumimasen ga, ashita wa man'in dess.	Sorry, but we're full tomorrow.
asatte	the day after tomorrow
dō	how about
Asatte wa dō dess ka?	How about the day after tomorrow?
daijōbu	all right
Asatte wa daijōbu dess.	The day after tomorrow is all right.
jā	well then
Jā, asatte yoyaku, o-negai shimahss.	Well then, please make the reservation for the day after tomorrow.
nan-mei-sama	how many people
-sama	polite equivalent to -*san*

Nan-mei-sama dess ka?	How many people?
futari	two people
Futari dess.	There are two people.
hitori	one person
kippu	ticket
ikura	how much
Kippu wa ikura dess ka?	How much is the ticket?
San-zen go-hyaku-en dess.	It's 3,500 yen.
O-namae wa?	What's your name?
Sumisu dess.	It's Smith.

UNIQUE ACCOMMODATIONS

If you want to experience lodging Japanese style, stay at a Japanese inn (**ryokan**). You'll be served a complete Japanese dinner and breakfast, and you'll sleep on bedding laid out on **tatami** (straw mat) floors. Or, try a **minshuku**, a family-run guesthouse offering lodging at a reasonable price.

For a unique experience, spend a night at a temple. Besides being able to sample the delicious and healthy temple cooking, you'll get a feel of the serenity and simplicity of temple living. Ask your travel agent or the Japan Travel Bureau for more information.

EXPRESSIONS IN CONTEXT

Kankō-basu no yoyaku, o-negai shimahss.	I'd like to make a reservation for the tour bus.
Itsu dess ka?	For when?
Kyō dess.	For today.
Asatte dess.	For the day after tomorrow.
Nan-mei-sama dess ka?	How many people are there?
Hitori dess.	One person.
O-namae wa?	What's your name?

Sumisu dess.	My name is Smith.
Kippu wa ikura dess ka?	How much is the ticket?
San-zen-en dess.	It's 3,000 yen.
Sumimasen ga, kyō wa man'in dess.	Sorry, but we're full for today.
Ashita wa dō dess ka?	How about tomorrow?
Ashita wa daijōbu dess.	Tomorrow is all right.
Jā, ashita, o-negai shimahss.	Well, then please make it for tomorrow.

LODGING FACILITIES

furonto	front desk; reception desk
robii	lobby
rōka	hall; corridor
erebētā	elevator
kaidan	stairs
shokudō	dining hall
o-furo	bath (communal bath)

RESERVATIONS AND CHECK-IN

heya	room
rūmu	room
shinguru-rūmu	single room
daburu-rūmu	double room
tsuin	twin room
basu-rūmu	bathroom
basu-tsuki no heya	room with a bathroom
ip-paku	overnight stay
ni-haku	two-night stay
Ni-haku shimahss.	We'll stay two nights.
san-paku	three-night stay

Motto yasui heya ga arimahss ka?	Do you have a cheaper room?
Motto ii heya ga arimahss ka?	Do you have a better room?
kagi	key
kōri	ice
Kōri, kudasai.	May I have some ice please?
san-nin	three people
yo-nin	four people
go-nin	five people

CHECK-OUT

o-kanjo	bill
ryōkin	charge
muryō	no charge
sābisu-ryō	service charge
zeikin	tax
uketori	receipt

OTHERS

Hachi-ji ni okoshite kudasai.	Please wake me at 8:00.
Kore o yūbin de dashite kudasai.	Please put this in the mail.
Kitte ga arimahss ka?	Do you have stamps?
Sentaku wa o-negai dekimahss ka?	Can I have this laundered?
reibō sōchi; eakon	air conditioner
Eakon no guai ga yokunai dess.	The air conditioner does not work very well.
danbō-sōchi; hiitā	heater
Danbō-sōchi ga yokunai dess.	The heater does not work very well.

CHAPTER 21
Help!

If you need help as you're wandering about on foot, go to a "police box" (**kōban**), usually located near train stations and street corners. Look for a small building with a policeman standing in front. The policemen on duty will gladly assist you in any way, even if it's just helping with directions.

WORDS & EXPRESSIONS

Tasukete!	Help!
Tasukete kudasai.	Please help me.
Komatte imahss.	I'm in trouble.
Dō shimashita ka?	What happened?
Byōki dess.	I'm sick.
kippu	ticket
o	(direct object particle)
nakushimashita	lost
Kippu o nakushimashita.	I lost my ticket.
densha ni	on the train
kamera	camera
Densha ni kamera o wasuremashita.	I forgot my camera on the train.
saifu	wallet
michi	way; road
ni mayoimashita	lost (the way)
Michi ni mayoimashita.	I lost my way.
hoteru	hotel
wa	(subject particle)
doko	where
wakarimasen	don't know; can't find

Hoteru wa doko ka wakarimasen.	I don't know where my hotel is.
koko	here; this place
Koko wa doko dess ka?	Where am I?
denwa	telephone
Denwa wa doko dess ka?	Where's a telephone?
kyūkyū-sha	ambulance
yonde kudasai	please call
Kyūkyū-sha o yonde kudasai.	Please call an ambulance.
Ei-go	English language
hanasu hito	person who speaks
Ei-go o hanasu hito o yonde kudasai.	Please call a person who speaks English.

USEFUL TELEPHONE NUMBERS

For travel information in English, call the Tourist Information Center (TIC). In Tokyo, their number is (03) 3201-3331; in Kyoto, (075) 344-3300; in Yokohama (045) 441-7300 and at Narita Airport, (0476) 34-5877 or (0476) 30-3383. For tourist information about eastern Japan and western Japan, dial toll-free 0120-444800 or 0088-224800. English directory assistance is 0120-364463.

For the police, dial 110 anywhere in the country. For reporting a fire or calling an ambulance, the number nationwide is 119.

EXPRESSIONS IN CONTEXT

Tasukete	Help!
Komatte imahss.	I'm in trouble.
Tasukete kudasai.	Please help me.
Dō shimashita ka?	What happened?
Byōki dess.	I'm sick.
Kyūkyū-sha o yonde kudasai.	Please call an ambulance.
Komatte imahss. Tasukete kudasai.	I'm in trouble. Please help me.

Dō shimashita ka?	What happened?
Michi ni mayoimashita.	I lost my way.
Hoteru wa doko dess ka?	Where's the hotel?
Denwa wa doko dess ka?	Where's a telephone?
Kippu o nakushimashita.	I lost my ticket.
Kamera o nakushimashita.	I lost my camera.
Densha ni saifu o wasuremashita.	I forgot my wallet on the train.
Wakarimasen.	I don't understand.
Ei-go o hanasu hito o yonde kudasai.	Please call a person who speaks English.

HEALTH

isha	doctor
Isha o yonde kudasai.	Please call a doctor.
Ei-go o hanasu isha	English-speaking doctor
kusuri	medicine
byōin	hospital
kango-fu	nurse
chūsha	injection; shot
kega	injury
taion-kei	thermometer
netsu	fever
Netsu ga arimahss.	I have a fever.
itai	hurt
atama	head
Atama ga itai dess.	My head hurts.
o-naka	stomach
ha	tooth
ashi	foot; leg
te	hand

harete imahss	swollen
Ashi ga harete imahss.	My foot is swollen.
mame	blister
Mame ga dekimashita.	I've developed a blister.
geri	diarrhea
Geri o shite imahss.	I've got diarrhea.
kaze	cold
kaze-gusuri	cold medicine
kaze o hiite imahss.	I have a cold.
Kono kusuri ga arimahss ka?	Do you have this medicine?
Nani-ka arimahss ka?	Do you have (some medicine) for me?
kanpō-yaku	Chinese medicine

OTHERS

o-kane	money
pasupōto	passport
toraberāzu-chekku	traveler's checks
Toraberāzu-chekku o nakushimashita.	I lost my traveler's checks.
ryōji-kan	consulate
taishi-kan	embassy
keisatsu-sho	police station
kōban	police box
dorobō	thief
Dorobō ni nusumaremashita.	I was robbed by a thief.

Dictionary

This dictionary has over 1,800 words and expressions needed for daily life in Japan. All entries appearing in the text have been included. Note that Japanese verbs are given in the polite (**-mahss**) present form. In the Japanese-English section, the honorific **o** for most nouns has been dropped. If you have difficulty finding a noun in the dictionary, check to see if it begiins with **o**. If it does, disregard this **o** and search for the word under its second letter. For example, in the dictionary, **o-hana** (flower) appears as **hana**.

ENGLISH-JAPANESE

admission fee nyūjō-ryō

admission ticket nyūjō-ken

adult otona

after ~ ato; ~ no ato

again mata

air conditioner reibō-sōchi; eakon

airplane hikō-ki

airport kūkō

alarm clock mezamashi-dokei

all right daijōbu

alone hitori

a.m. gozen

ambulance kyūkyū-sha

America Amerika

American (person) Amerika-jin

amusement park yūen-chi

animal dōbutsu

anniversary kinen-bi

antique kottō(-hin)

apple ringo

appointment yakusoku

April Shi-gatsu

archway (Shinto shrine) torii

arrival time tōchaku-jikan

at de

August Hachi-gatsu

Australia Ōsutoraria

Australian (person) Ōsutoraria-jin

autumn aki

bad warui

bag; baggage nimotsu

baggage checkroom te-nimotsu ichiji azukari-jo

bakery pan-ya

bamboo shoot takenoko

bank ginkō

banquet enkai

bar bā
baseball yakyū
baseball game yakyū no shiai
basement chika
bath o-furo
bathroom basu-rūmu; o-tearai
bean paste miso
beautiful utsukushii
beef gyū-niku
beer biiru
before ~ mae; ~ no mae (ni)
behind ~ ushiro; ~ no ushiro (ni)
beverage nomi-mono
big ōkii
bird tori
birthday tanjō-bi
bitter nigai
black tea kōcha
boarding area; landing nori-ba
book hon
bookstore hon-ya
borrow (verb) karimahss
  please borrow karite kudasai
botanical garden shokubutsu-en
bought kaimashita
bound for ~ -yuki
box lunch bentō
box lunch (sold at a station) eki-ben
boy otoko no ko

breakfast asa-gohan
break into small money (verb)
  kuzushimahss
  please break into small money
  kuzushite kudasai
break-up; disperse (verb) kaisan
  shimahss
break-up time; dispersal time
  kaisan-jikan
bright azayaka
brother (see older brother, younger
  brother)
buckwheat noodle o-soba
Buddha Hotoke-sama; Oshaka-sama
Buddha (large statue of) daibutsu
Buddhist temple o-tera
building biru
bullet train Shinkansen
bus basu
bus stop basu-teiryūjo; basu-tei
buy (verb) kaimahss
  doesn't buy; don't buy kaimasen
  please buy katte kudasai

cabbage kyabetsu
calendar karendā
call (verb) yobimahss
  please call yonde kudasai
camera kamera

camera shop kamera-ya
camping kyanpu
can; is able dekimahss
Canada Kanada
Canadian (person) Kanada-jin
can't; isn't able dekimasen
car kuruma
carrot ninjin
castle shiro
cat neko
catch a cold (verb) kaze o hikimahss
cell phone keitai-denwa
Celsius Sesshi
Certainly, sir/ma'am. Kashikomarima-shita.
charge; fee ryōkin
check; bill o-kanjō
checkers (Japanese board game) go
check-out time chekku-auto taimu
chicken tori-niku
child; children kodomo
China Chūgoku
chinaware; ceramics tōjiki
Chinese (language) Chūgoku-go
Chinese (person) Chūgoku-jin
Chinese cuisine Chūgoku-ryōri
chopsticks o-hashi
church kyōkai
city; town machi

climate kikō
clock tokei
cloisonné shippō-yaki
closing hour of a store heiten-jikan
cloth (for wrapping) furoshiki
cloth; textile ori-mono
cloudy kumori
Coca-Cola Koka-kōra
cocktail party kakuteru-pātii
coffee kōhii
coffee shop kissa-ten
cold (sickness) kaze
cold (temperature) samui
cold (to the touch) tsumetai
cold day samui hi
cold medicine kaze-gusuri
college; university daigaku
come (verb) kimahss
  please come kite kudasai
company kaisha
company employee kaisha-in
concert konsāto
conductor (train) shashō
conference; meeting kaigi
Congratulations! Omedetō gozaimahss!
consulate ryōji-kan
cookie kukki
cool suzushii
corn tōmorokoshi

corner kado
country; rural area inaka
crab kani
credit card kurejitto-kādo
cucumber kyūri
cup; glass koppu
curry with rice karē-raisu
customer o-kyaku

daughter (one's own) musume
daughter (someone else's) musume-san
day after tomorrow asatte
day before yesterday ototoi
day off holiday yasumi
December Jū-ni-gatsu
deer shika
degree do
delicious; tasty oishii
dentist ha-isha
department store depāto
departure time shuppatsu-jikan
diarrhea geri
did shimashita
different; another hoka
different one hoka-no
dining car shokudō-sha
dining hall shokudō
do (verb) shimahss
   doesn't do; don't do shimasen

   please do shite kudasai
doctor isha
dog inu
doll ningyō
door doa
double room daburu-rūmu
down shita
drink (verb) nomimahss
   please drink nonde kudasai
drink; beverage nomi-mono

early hayaku
east higashi
eat (verb) tabemahss
   please eat tabete kudasai
egg tamago
eggplant nasu
eight hachi; yattsu
eighth day of the month yōka
electrical goods denki-seihin
elevator erebētā
embassy taishi-kan
England Igirisu
English (language) Ei-go
English (person) Igirisu-jin
entrance iriguchi
escalator esukarētā
evening yūgata
everyday mai-nichi

every night mai-ban
every month mai-tsuki; mai-getsu
every week mai-shū
every year mai-nen; mai-toshi
exchange money (verb) ryō-gae
shimahss
please exchange money ryō-gae shite
kudasai
excursion boat yūran-sen
Excuse me. Sumimasen.
exhibition tenran-kai
exit deguchi
expensive takai
exposition hakuran-kai
express train kyūkō
expressway kōsoku-dōro
extension naisen

Fahrenheit Kashi
fall (verb, used for rain, snow) furimahss
it rains ame ga furimahss
it snows yuki ga furimahss
famous yūmei
far tōi
fare unchin; ryōkin
fare table/listing unchin-hyō
farewell party sōbetsu-kai
father (one's own) chichi
father (someone else's; and when

addressing one's own) otōsan
February Ni-gatsu
female onna; josei
ferry boat ferii
festival o-matsuri
fever netsu
field trip; tour of a factory kengaku-
ryokō
fifth day of the month itsuka
film firumu
fine rippa
fine; healthy genki
fine weather hare
fireworks hanabi
fireworks display hanabi-taikai
first day of the month tsuitachi
fish sakana
five go; itsutsu
flashy; gaudy hade
floor yuka
floor (story) kai
fog kiri
folding fan sensu
folding screen byōbu
folk-art handicraft mingei-hin
for; of no
forget (verb) wasuremahss
please forget wasurete kudasai
fork fōku

four shi/yon; yottsu
fourth day of the month yokka
France Furansu
free; no charge muryō
French (language) Furansu-go
French (person) Furansu-jin
Friday Kin-yōbi
friend tomodachi
front desk; reception desk furonto
fruit kuda-mono; furūtsu
full ippai
full; no vacancy man'in
funeral o-sōshiki

gallery garō
game; match; tournament shiai
garden niwa
gas station gifuto-shoppu;
  miyagemono-ya
gate (temple) sanmon
gaudy; flashy hade
Germany Doitsu
German (language) Doitsu-go
German (person) Doitsu-jin
get up (verb) okimahss
  please get up okite kudasai
gift shop gifuto-shoppu; miyagemono-ya
girl onna no ko
Glad to meet you. Dōzo yoroshiku.

go (verb) ikimahss
  doesn't go; don't go ikimasen
  please go itte kudasai
golf gorufu
golf tournament gorufu no konpe
good ii
Good afternoon./Hello. Konnichiwa.
Goodbye. Sayōnara.
Good evening. Konbanwa.
Good morning. Ohayō gozaimahss.
Good night. Oyasumi-nasai.
grandchild (one's own) mago
grandchild (someone else's) o-mago-san
grape budō
green light ao-shingō
green tea o-cha
group tour dantai-ryokō
guesthouse; inn (family-run) minshuku
guidebook gaido-bukku

half han
hall; corridor rōka
hand te
hard; tough katai
have (verb) arimahss
he kare
head atama
healthy; fine genki
hear (be able to) kikoemahss

hear; listen (verb) kikimahss
　please hear kiite kudasai
heater danbō-sōchi; hiitā
heavy omoi
Hello. (on the telephone) Moshi-moshi.
Hello./Good afternoon. Konnichiwa.
help (verb) tasukemahss
　please help tasukete kudasai
here; this place koko
hiking haikingu
historical site shiseki
hobby shumi
holiday; day-off yasumi
holiday (national) saijitsu
hospital byōin
hot atsui
hot day atsui hi
hotel hoteru
hot spring onsen
how about ikaga
How are you?/Are you well? O-genki
　dess ka?
How do you do? Hajimemashite.
how; in what way dōshite
how many ikutsu
how much ikura
humid mushi-atsui
hungry (to be) o-naka ga suite imahss
hurt itai

I watashi
ice kōri
ice cream aisu-kuriimu
Imari ware Imari-yaki
Imperial Hotel Teikoku Hoteru
Imperial Palace Kōkyo
in; at de
in; inside naka
Indonesia Indoneshia
Indonesian (language) Indoneshia-go
Indonesian (person) Indoneshia-jin
in English Ei-go de
inexpensive yasui
information office annai-jo
injection; shot chūsha
injury kega
Inland Sea Seto-naikai
inn; guesthouse minshuku
inn (traditional) ryokan
international telephone call kokusai-
　denwa
intersection kōsaten
is; am; are dess
isn't; am not; aren't dewa arimasen
isn't it?/aren't you? ne
Italian (language) Itaria-go
Italian (person) Itaria-jin
Italy Itaria

January Ichi-gatsu
Japanese (language) Nihon-go
Japanese (person) Nihon-jin
Japanese cuisine Nihon-ryōri
Japanese inn ryokan
Japanese wrestling sumō
July Shichi-gatsu
June Roku-gatsu

Kabuki kabuki
Kabuki Theater Kabuki-za
key kagi
kimono kimono
kimono (light, cotton) yukata
kiosk; station shop kiosuku; eki no baiten
Korea (rok) Kankoku
Korean (language) Kankoku-go
Korean (person) Kankoku-jin

lacquerware nuri-mono
lake mizuumi
lantern chōchin
last month sengetsu
last week senshū
last year kyonen
late osoi
laundry sentaku-mono
lawyer bengo-shi

leave; go out (verb) dekakemahss; demahss
   please leave dete kudasai
left hidari
leg ashi
lend (verb) kashimahss
   please lend kashite kudasai
let off (verb) oroshimahss
   please let (me) off oroshite kudasai
letter tegami
lettuce retasu
library tosho-kan
light karui
lightning inazuma
like; be fond of suki
limited-express ticket tokkyū-ken
limited-express train tokkyū
line (train) sen
listen (verb) kikimahss
   please listen kiite kudasai
lobby robii
local telephone call shinai-denwa
local train futsū
long-distance telephone call chōkyori-denwa
look (verb) mimahss
   please look mite kudasai
looked mimashita
lose (verb) nakushimahss

lose the way (verb) michi ni mayoimahss
lotus root renkon
lunch hiru-gohan

magazine zasshi
mahjong mājan
mail (a letter) yūbin de dashimahss
  please mail yūbin de dashite kudasai
male otoko
man otoko no hito
many; much takusan
map chizu
March San-gatsu
May Go-gatsu
meal gohan; shokuji
meal (meal included) shokuji-tsuki
meat niku
medicine kusuri
meeting; conference kaigi
meeting time shūgō-jikan
melon meron
message messēji
milk gyūnyū
minute (suffix used for) -fun
moment; awhile shibaraku
Monday Getsu-yōbi
money o-kane
monorail monorēru
monument kinen-hi

moon viewing tsuki-mi
more motto
morning asa
mother (one's own) haha
mother (someone else's; and when addressing one's own) okāsan
mountain yama
mountain climbing yama-nobori
Mount Fuji Fuji-san
movie eiga
movie theater eiga-kan
Mr. /Mrs. /Ms. /Miss -san
museum hakubutsu-kan
mushroom shiitake

name namae
napkin napukin
national holiday saijitsu
near chikai
nearby soba
new; fresh atarashii
newspaper shinbun
next month raigetsu
next week raishū
next year rainen
night yoru
nine kyū/ku; kokonotsu
ninth day of the month kokonoka
no iie

No, thank you. Kekkō dess.
nonsmoking car kin'en-sha
noodle (dark and thin) soba
noodle (white and fat) udon
noon hiru
north kita
November Jū-ichi-gatsu
now ima
nurse kango-fu

occupation; work shigoto
ocean umi
o'clock (suffix used for) -ji
October Jū-gatsu
octopus tako
of; for no
old (not young) toshi-totta
old; stale furui
older brother (one's own) ani
older brother (someone else's; and when addressing one's own) oniisan
older sister (one's own) ane
older sister (someone else's; and when addressing one's own) onēsan
once more mō ichido
one ichi; hitotsu
one hundred hyaku
one person hitori
one thousand sen

one-thousand yen note sen-en-satsu
one-way (ticket) katamichi(-kippu)
onion tamanegi
opening hour of a store kaiten-jikan
orange orenji
orange juice orenji-jūsu
out; outside soto
overnight stay ip-paku
over there asoko
oyster bed kaki-yōshokujo

Pacific Ocean Taihei-yō
pagoda; tower tō
painting e
paper kami
paper (traditional, handmade) washi
park kōen
parking lot chūsha-jō
party pātii
passport pasupōto
peace heiwa
peach momo
pearl shinju
persimmon kaki
person hito
pharmacy kusuri-ya; yakkyoku
photo shashin
physical exercise undō
pickle tsuke-mono

picnic pikunikku
picture e
place of interest meisho
plain; open field heiya
plate sara
platform hōmu
please dozō; kudasai; o-negai shimahss
p.m. gogo
police keisatsu
police box kōban
police station keisatu-sho
poor; unskillful heta
pork buta-niku
pork cutlet ton-katsu
Portugal Porutogaru
Portuguese (language) Porutogaru-go
Portuguese (person) Porutogaru-jin
postcard e-hagaki; hagaki
post office yūbin-kyoku
potato jagaimo
pottery seto-mono
prefecture ken
pretty kirei
previous day mae no hi
price nedan
promise; appointment yakusoku
public square hiro-ba
public telephone kōshū-denwa
pumpkin kabocha

quickly hayaku

radio rajio
rain ame
raw nama
read (verb) yomimahss
  please read yonde kudasai
receipt uketori; ryōshū-sho
reception desk uketsuke; furonto
redcap; porter akabō
regional specialty meisan
reporter; journalist kisha
reservation yoyaku
reserved-seat ticket zaseki shitei-ken
restaurant resutoran
restroom o-tearai
return an object (verb) kaeshimahss
  please return kaeshite kudasai
return home (verb) kaerimahss
  please return home kaette kudasai
rice kome; gohan; raisu
rice (cooked) gohan; raisu
rice bowl chawan
rice cracker senbei
rice paddy suiden
right migi
right away sugu
river kawa
road michi; dōro

robbed (to be) nusumaremahss
roof okujō
room heya; rūmu
room with a bath basu-tsuki no heya
round marui
round-trip (ticket) ōfuku(-kippu)
Russia Roshia
Russian (language) Roshia-go
Russian (person) Roshia-jin

saké o-sake
saké cup sakazuki
salad sarada
salty shoppai
Saturday Do-yōbi
saw mimashita
say (verb) iimahss
  please say itte kudasai
scroll (hanging) kake-mono
sculpture chōkoku
season kisetsu
seaweed nori
second day of the month futsuka
secretary hisho
see (verb) mimahss
  doesn't see; don't see mimasen
  please see mite kudasai
See you later. Jā mata.
send (verb) okurimahss

  please send okutte kudasai
separately betsu-betsu ni
September Ku-gatsu
service charge sābisu-ryō
set meal teishoku
seven shichi/nana; nanatsu
seventh day of the month nanoka
she kanojo
Shinto shrine jinja
ship fune
show (verb) misemahss
  please show misete kudasai
shower (bath) shawā
shower (rain) niwaka-ame
shrimp ebi
sickness byōki
sightseeing kankō
sightseeing bus kankō-basu
signal shingō
silk kinu
single room shinguru-rūmu
sister (see older sister, younger sister)
six roku; muttsu
sixth day of the month muika
skyscraper kōsō-biru
sleep; go to bed (verb) nemahss
  please sleep/go to bed nete kudasai
slowly yukkuri
small chiisai

smog sumoggu
snow yuki
so sō
soft; tender yawarakai
son (one's own) musuko
son(someone else's) musuko-san
soon; shortly mō sugu
Sorry, but... Sumimasen ga...
soup (Japanese) sui-mono
soup (Western) sūpu
south minami
souvenir o-miyage
Spain Supein
Spanish (language) Supein-go
Spanish (person) Supein-jin
speak (verb) hanashimahss
  please speak hanashite kudasai
spicy karai
spoon supūn
sport supōtsu
spring (season) haru
square shikakui
stadium sutajiamu
stairs kaidan
stamp (postal) kitte
start (verb) hajimarimahss; hajimemahss
  please start hajimete kudasai
station eki
station employee eki-in

station shop kiosuku; eki no baiten
statue zō
statue of Buddha butsuzō
steak sutēki
steal (verb) nusumimahss
stomach o-naka
stop (a car) tomarimahss; tomemahss
  please stop tomete kudasai
store mise
storm arashi
student gakusei
subway chika-tetsu
subway station chika-tetsu no eki
sukiyaki suki-yaki
summer natsu
summer vacation natsu-yasumi
sumo sumō
Sunday Nichi-yōbi
supper ban-gohan
sushi o-sushi
swell (verb) haremahss

take (verb) torimahss
  please take totte kudasai
take a photo shashin o torimahss
tangerine mikan
taste aji
tasty; delicious oishii
tasty; (not); unappetizing mazui

tax zeikin
taxi takushii
taxi stand takushii-noriba
tea (black) kōcha
tea (green) o-cha
teach (verb) oshiemahss
  please teach oshiete kudasai
teacher sensei
teacup yu-nomi
tea field cha-batake
teatime o-cha no jikan
telephone denwa
telephone (verb) denwa shimahss
  please telephone denwa shite
  kudasai
telephone book denwa-chō
telephone card terefon-kādo
telephone charge/bill denwa-ryō
telephone number denwa-bangō
telephone operator kōkan-shu
television terebi
temperature ondo
temple o-tera
tempura tenpura
ten jū; tō
tenth day of the month tōka
ten thousand ichi-man
Thai (language) Tai-go
Thai (person) Tai-jin

Thialand Tai
Thank you. Arigatō./Dōmo arigatō.
Thank you. (I'll have some.)
  Itadakimahss.
Thank you. (It was delicious.)
  Gochisō-sama deshita.
that sono; ano
that (pronoun) sore; are
theater geki-jō
there is/are; (for animate objects)
  imahss
there is/are; have (for inanimate
  objects) arimahss
thermometer taion-kei
thief dorobō
third day of the month mikka
this kono
this (pronoun) kore
this month kongetsu
this week konshū
this year kotoshi
three san; mittsu
thunder kaminari
Thursday Moku-yōbi
ticket kippu
ticket machine (kippu no) jidō-
  hanbaiki
time a performance starts kaimaku-
  jikan

tip chippu
to e
to; as far as made
today kyō
tofu tōfu
Tokyo Station Tōkyō Eki
Tokyo Tower Tōkyō Tawā
tomato tomato
tomorrow ashita
tomorrow morning ashita no asa
tonight; this evening kon-ban
tooth ha
tour tsuā
tour (of a city) shinai-kankō
tourist kankō-kyaku
towel (bath towel) basu-taoru
towel (hot or cold hand towel)
   o-shibori
town; city machi
track number ~ ~ -ban-sen
traditional dentō-teki
train densha; ressha
transfer nori-kae
travel ryokō
travel (verb) ryokō shimahss
travel bureau ryokō-sentā
traveler ryokō-sha
traveler's check toraberāzu-chekku
travel insurance ryokō-hoken

trouble (I'm in trouble.) komatte
   imahss
trunk (of a car) toranku
Tuesday Ka-yōbi
tuna maguro
turn (verb) magarimahss; magemahss
   please turn magatte kudasai
twin room tsuin
two ni; futatsu
two people futari
typhoon taifū

Ueno Park Ueno Kōen
umbrella kasa
unappetizing mazui
understand (verb) wakarimahss
   doesn't/don't understand wakarimasen
United States Amerika
university; college daigaku
up ue

vegetable yasai
vending machine jidō-hanbaiki
vicinity hen
Vietnam Betonamu
Vietnamese (language) Betonamu-go
Vietnamese (person) Betonamu-jin

wait (verb) machimahss
  please wait matte kudasai
waiting room machiai-shitsu
wake someone up (verb) okoshimahss
  please wake me up okoshite kudasai
wake up okimahss
  please wake up okite kudasai
walk (a stroll) sanpo
walk (verb) arukimahss
  please walk aruite kudasai
wallet saifu
want hoshii
want to buy kai-tai dess
want to do shi-tai dess
want to drink nomi-tai dess
want to eat tabe-tai dess
want to go iki-tai dess
want to see mi-tai dess
war sensō
warm atatakai
was deshita
wash (verb) araimahss
  please wash aratte kudasai
wash clothes (verb) sentaku shimahss
  please wash clothes sentaku shite kudasai
watch; clock tokei
watch; see mimahss
  please watch mite kudasai

watch shop tokei-ya
water mizu
watermelon suika
weather tenki
weather bureau kishō-dai
weather forecast tenki-yohō
wedding ceremony kekkon-shiki
Wednesday Sui-yōbi
weekday heijitsu
weekend shūmatsu
welcome party kangei-kai
well; nicely yoku
well... sā...
went ikimashita
west nishi
Western cuisine Seiyō-ryōri
what nan (i)
what (with what) nan de
what day of the month nan-nichi
what day of the week nan-yōbi
what month nan-gatsu
what time nan-ji
what year nan-nen
when itsu
where doko
which dore
whiskey uisukii
whiskey and water mizu-wari
who dare; dochira-sama

wicket kaisatsu-guchi
will be; would be; will probably be deshō
wind kaze
wind chime fūrin
window mado
wine wain
winter fuyu
winter vacation fuyu-yasumi
with what nan de
woman onna no hito
wonderful subarashii
woodblock print hanga
work; occupation shigoto
work (verb) hatarakimahss
wrap (verb) tsutsumimahss
  please wrap tsutsunde kudasai
write (verb) kakimahss
  please write kaite kudasai
writer sakka
wrong chigaimahss
wrong number bangō-chigai

year after next sarai-nen
year before last ototoshi
yes hai
yesterday kinō
yogurt yōguruto
you anata

You're welcome. Dō-itashimashite.
younger brother (one's own) otōto
younger brother (someone else's) otōto-san
younger sister (one's own) imōto
younger sister (someone else's) imōto-san
your anata no

zoo dōbutsu-en

JAPANESE-ENGLISH

aisu-kuriimu ice cream
aji taste
akabō redcap; porter
aka-shingō red light
akemahss open (verb)
aki autumn
amai sweet
ame rain
Amerika America
Amerika-jin American (person)
anata you
anata no your
ane older sister (one's own)
ani older brother (one's own)
annai-jo information office
ano that
ao-shingō green light
araimahss wash (verb)
arashi storm
are that (pronoun)
arigatō thank you
arimasen there isn't /aren't (for inanimate objects)
arimahss there is/are (for inanimate objects)
arukimashita walked
arukimahss walk (verb)
asa morning

asa-gohan breakfast
asatte day after tomorrow
ashi foot; leg
ashita no asa tomorrow morning
ashita no gogo tomorrow afternoon
asoko over there
atama head
atarashii new; fresh
atatakai warm
atsui hot
atsui hi hot day
azayaka bright

bā bar
bangō-chigai wrong number
ban-gohan supper
~ -ban-sen track number ~
basu bus
basu-rūmu bathroom; restroom
basu-taoru bath towel
basu-tei bus stop
basu-tsuki no heya room with a bath
bengo-shi lawyer
Betonamu Vietnam
Betonamu-go Vietnamese (language)
Betonamu-jin Vietnamese (person)
betsu-betsu separately
biiru beer
biru building

bonsai miniature potted tree or shrub
budō grape
buta-niku pork
butsuzō statue of Buddha
buzā buzzer
byōbu folding screen
byōin hospital
byōki sickness

cha green tea
cha-batake tea field
chawan rice bowl
chekku-auto taimu check-out time
chichi father (one's own)
chigaimahss wrong
chiisai small
chika basement
chikai near
chikai uchi ni one of these days
chika-tetsu subway
chika-tetsu no eki subway station
chippu tip
chizu map
chōchin lantern
chōkoku sculpture
chōkyori-denwa long-distance
    telephone call
chotto just a little; just a moment
Chūgoku China

Chūgoku-go Chinese (language)
Chūgoku-jin Chinese (person)
Chūgoku-ryōri Chinese cuisine
chūsha injection; shot
chūsha-jō parking lot

daburu-rūmu double room
daibutsu large statue of Buddha
daigaku college; university
daijōbu all right
danbō-sōchi heater
dantai-ryokō group tour
dare who
de at; in; with
deguchi exit
dekakemahss leave; go out (verb)
dekimasen can't; isn't able
dekimahss can; is able
demahss leave; go out (verb)
denki-seihin electrical goods
densha train
dentō-teki traditional
denwa telephone
denwa-bangō telephone number
denwa-chō telephone book
denwa-ryō telephone charge/bill
denwa shimahss telephone (verb)
depāto department store
deshita was; were

deshō will be; would be; will probably be

dess is; am; are

dewa arimasen isn't; am not; aren't

do degree

dō how

doa door

dōbutsu animal

dōbutsu-en zoo

dochira-sama who (polite)

Dō-itashimashite. You're welcome.

Doitsu Germany (country)

Doitsu-go German (language)

Doitsu-jin German (people)

doko where

dōmo thanks

dōmo arigatō thank you

donna what kind of

dore which

dōro road

dorobō thief

dōshite how

Do-yōbi Saturday

dōzo please

Dōzo yoroshiku. Glad to meet you.

e picture

e to

ebi shrimp

e-hagaki postcard

eiga movie

eiga-kan movie theater

Ei-go English (language)

Ei-go de in English

eki station

eki-ben box lunch sold at stations

eki-in station employee

eki no baiten station shop

enkai banquet

erebētā elevator

esukarētā escalator

ferii ferryboat

firumu film (roll of)

fōku fork

Fuji-san Mount Fuji

-fun minute (suffix used for)

fune ship

Furansu France

Furansu-go French (language)

Furansu-jin French (person)

furimahss fall (verb, used for rain, snow)

fūrin wind chime

furo bath

furonto front desk; reception desk

furoshiki cloth used for wrapping things

furui old; stale
fusuma sliding screen
futari two people
futatsu two (objects)
futsū local train
futsū ordinary
futsuka second day of the month
fuyu winter
fuyu-yasumi winter vacation

ga (subject particle)
gaido-bukku guidebook
gakusei student
garō gallery
gasorin-sutando gas station
geki-jō theater
genki healthy; fine
geri diarrhea
Getsu-yōbi Monday
gifuto-shoppu gift shop
ginkō bank
Ginza (place name in Tokyo)
go five
go Japanese board game
Gochisō-sama deshita. Thank you.
  (It was delicious.)
Go-gatsu May
gogo p.m.
gohan meal; cooked rice

gorufu golf
-gō-sha car # ~
gozen a.m.
gyū-niku beef
gyū-nyū milk

ha tooth
hachi eight
Hachi-gatsu August
hade flashy; gaudy
hagaki postcard
haha mother (one's own)
hai yes
haikingu hiking
ha-isha dentist
hajimarimahss start (verb)
Hajimemashite. How do you do?
hajimemahss start (verb)
hakubutsu-kan museum
hakuran-kai exposition
han half
hanabi fireworks
hanabi-taikai fireworks display
hanashimahss speak (verb)
hanga woodblock print
hare fine weather
haremahss swell (verb)
haru spring (season)
hashi chopsticks

hatarakimahss work (verb)
hayaku early; quickly
heijitsu weekday
heiten-jikan hour a store closes
heiwa peace
heiya plain; open field
hen vicinity
heta poor; unskillful
heya room
hidari left
higashi east
hikimahss catch (a cold); pull (verb)
hikō-ki airplane
hiro-ba public square
hiru noon
hiru-gohan lunch
hisho secretary
hito person
hitori one person; alone
hitotsu one (object)
hoka-no different one
hōmu platform
hon book
hon-ya bookstore
hoshii want
hoteru hotel
Hotoke-sama Buddha
hyaku hundred

ichi one
Ichi-gatsu January
ichi-man ten thousand
Igirisu England
Igirisu-jin English (person)
ii good
iie no
iimahss say (verb)
ika cuttlefish
ikaga how about
ikimasen doesn't go; don't go
ikimashita went
ikimahss go (verb)
ikura how much
ikutsu how many
ima now
Imari-yaki Imari ware
imasen there isn't/aren't (for animate objects)
imahss there is/are (for animate objects)
imōto younger sister (one's own)
imōto-san younger sister (someone else's)
inaka country; rural area
inazuma lightning
Indoneshia Indonesia
Indoneshia-go Indonesian (language)
Indoneshia-jin Indonesian (person)
inu dog
ippai full; no vacancy

ip-paku overnight stay
iriguchi entrance
isha doctor
Itadakimahss. Thank you. (I'll have some.)
itai hurt
Itaria Italy
Itaria-go Italian (language)
Itaria-jin Italian (person)
itsu when
itsuka fifth day of the month
itsutsu five (objects)
itte kudasai please say

jagaimo potato
Jā mata. See you later.
-ji o'clock/hours (suffix for)
jidō-hanbaiki vending machine
jikoku-hyo timetable
jimi subdued; refined
jinja Shinto shrine
jiyū-seki nonreserved seat
jū ten
jūdo jūdo (Japanese art of self-defense)
Jū-gatsu October
Jū-ichi-gatsu November
Jū-ni-gatsu December

ka (question particle)

kabocha pumpkin
kabuki Kabuki; Kabuki performance
Kabuki-za Kabuki Theater
kado corner
kaerimahss return home (verb)
kaeshimahss return an object (verb)
kagi key
kai floor (story)
kaidan stairs
kaigai ryokō overseas travel
kaigi meeting; conference
kaimaku-jikan time a performance starts
kaimasen doesn't buy; don't buy
kaimashita bought
kaimahss buy (verb)
kaisan-jikan break-up time
kaisan shimahss breakup; disperse (verb)
kaisatsu-guchi wicket
kaisha-in company employee
kaiten-jikan opening hour of a store
kake-mono hanging scroll
kaki persimmon
kakimahss write (verb)
kaki-yōshokujō oyster bed
kakuteru-pātii cocktail party
kamera camera
kamera-ya camera shop
kami paper
kaminari thunder

Kanada Canada
Kanada-jin Canadian (person)
Kanda (place name in Tokyo)
kane money
kangei-kai welcome party
kango-fu nurse
kani crab
kanjō check; bill
kankō sightseeing
kankō-basu sightseeing bus
Kankoku Korea (ROK)
Kankoku-go Korean (language)
Kankoku-jin Korean (person)
kankō-kyaku tourist
kanojo she
kanpō-yaku Chinese medicine
karai spicy
karendā calendar
karē-raisu curry with rice
karimahss borrow (verb)
karui light
kasa umbrella
kashi sweets
Kashi Fahrenheit
Kashikomarimashita. Certainly, sir/ma'am.
kashimahss lend (verb)
kashite kudasai please lend it
katai hard; tough

katamichi (-kippu) one-way (ticket)
kawa river
Ka-yōbi Tuesday
kaze cold (sickness)
kaze wind
kaze-gusuri cold medicine
kaze o hikimahss catch a cold (verb)
kega injury
keisatsu police
keisatsu-sho police station
kēki cake
Kekkō dess. No, thank you.
kekkon-shiki wedding ceremony
ken prefecture
kenbutsu sightseeing
kengaku-ryokō field trip; tour of a factory, institution, etc.
kikimahss hear; listen (verb)
kikō climate
kikoemahss can hear
kimono kimono; Japanese clothes
kinen-bi anniversary
kinen-hi monument
kin'en-sha nonsmoking car
kinō yesterday
kinu silk
Kin-yōbi Friday
kiosuku kiosk; station shop
kippu ticket

kirei pretty
kiri fog
kisetsu season
kisha reporter; journalist
kishō-dai weather bureau
kissa-ten coffee shop
kita north
kitte stamp
kōban police box
kōcha black tea
kodomo child; children
kōen park
kōhii coffee
Koka-kōra Coca-Cola
kōkan-shu telephone operator
koko here; this place
kokonoka ninth day of the month
kokonotsu nine (objects)
kokusai-denwa international telephone call
Kōkyo Imperial Palace
Komatte imahss. I'm in trouble.
kome rice
konban tonight; this evening
Konbanwa. Good evening.
kongetsu this month
Konnichiwa. Hello./Good afternoon.
kono this
konsāto concert

konshū this week
koppu cup; glass
kore this (pronoun)
korekuto-kōru collect call
kōri ice
kōsaten intersection
kōshū-denwa public phone
kōsō-biru skyscraper
kōsoku-dōro expressway
kotoshi this year
kottō(-hin) antique
ku nine
kuda-mono fruit
kudasai please; please give me
Ku-gatsu September
kukkii cookie
kūkō airport
kumori cloudy
kurejitto-kādo credit card
kuruma car
kusuri medicine
kusuri-ya pharmacy
kuzushimahss break into small money (verb)
kyabetsu cabbage
kyaku customer
kyanpu camping
kyō today
kyōkai church

kyonen last year
kyū nine
kyūka day off
kyūkō express train
kyūkyū-sha ambulance
kyūri cucumber

machi town; city
machiai-shitsu waiting room
machimahss wait (verb)
made to; as far as
mado window
mae before
mae no hi previous day
magarimahss turn (verb)
mago grandchild (one's own)
maguro tuna
mai-ban every night
mai-getsu every month
mai-nen every year
mai-nichi everyday
mai-shū every week
mai-tsuki every month
mājan mahjong
mame blister
man'in full; no vacancy
manjū bun with bean-jam filling
marui round
mata again

matsuri festival
mayoimahss lose the way
mazui not tasty
meisan regional specialty
meisho place of interest; tourist spot
meron melon
messēji message
mezamashi-dokei alarm clock
michi way; road
migi right
mikan tangerine
mikka third day of the month
mimasen doesn't see; don't see
mimashita saw
mimahss see; look; watch (verb)
minami south
mingei-hin folk-art handicraft
minshuku family-run guesthouse/inn
mise store
misemahss show (verb)
miso bean paste
mittsu three (objects)
miyage souvenir
mizu water
mizuumi lake
mizu-wari whiskey and water
mō ichido once more
Moku-yōbi Thursday
momo peach

monorēru monorail
Moshi-moshi. Hello. (on the telephone)
mō sugu soon; shortly
motto more; some more
muika sixth day of the month
muryō no charge
mushi-atsui humid
musuko son (one's own son)
musuko-san son (someone else's)
musume daughter (one's own)
musume-san daughter (someone else's)
muttsu six (objects)

naisen extension
naka in; inside
nakushimahss lose (verb)
nama raw
namae name
nan(i) what
nana seven
nanatsu seven (objects)
nan de with what
nan-gatsu what month
nan-ji what time
nan-nen what year
nanoka the seventh
napukin napkin
nashi pear
nasu eggplant

natsu summer
natsu-yasumi summer vacation
ne isn't it?/aren't you?
nedan price
neko cat
nemahss go to bed; sleep (verb)
netsu fever
ni at; in; on
ni two
Nichi-yōbi Sunday
nigai bitter
Ni-gatsu February
nigiri-zushi, ichinin-mae set order of
   sushi for one peson
Nihon-go Japanese (language)
Nihon-jin Japanese (person)
Nihon-yōri Japanese cuisine
Nikkō (place name)
niku meat
nimotsu bag; baggage
ningyō doll
ninjin carrot
nishi west
nishoku-tsuki two meals included
niwa garden
niwaka-ame shower (rain)
no of; for
~ no ato (de) after ~
~ no mae (ni) before ~

nomimahss drink (verb)
nomi-mono drink; beverage
nori seaweed
nori-ba boarding area; landing
nori-kae transfer
nuri-mono lacquerware
nusumimahss steal (verb)
nyūjō-ken admission ticket
nyūjō-ryō admission fee

o (direct object particle)
o- (honorific prefix)
o-cha no jikan teatime
ōfuku (-kippu) round-trip (ticket)
O-genki dess ka? How are you? /Are you well?
Ohayō gozaimahss. Good morning.
oishii delicious
okāsan mother (someone else's; and when addressing one's own)
ōkii big
ōkii-no big one
okimahss get up (verb)
okoshimahss wake someone up (verb)
okujō roof
okurimahss send (verb)
o-machi kudasai please wait
o-mago-san grandchild (someone else's)
Omedetō gozaimahss! Congratulations!

omoi heavy
o-naka stomach
O-naka ga suite imahss. I'm hungry.
O-namae wa? What's your name?
ondo temperature
o-negai shimahss please
onēsan older sister (someone else's; and when addressing one's own)
oniisan older brother (someone else's; and when addressing one's own)
onna female
onna no hito woman
onna no ko girl
onsen hot spring
orenji orange
orenji-jūsu orange juice
ori-mono cloth; textile
oroshimahss let off (verb)
o-shibori hot or cold hand towel used for wiping one's hands
oshiemahss teach; tell (verb)
osoku late
Ōsutoraria Australia
Ōsutoraria-jin Australian (person)
o-tearai restroom; bathroom
otoko male
otoko no hito man
otoko no ko boy
otona adult

otōsan father (someone else's; and when addressing one's own)

otōto younger brother (one's own)

ototoi day before yesterday

otōto-san younger brother (someone else's)

ototoshi year before last

Oyasumi-nasai. Good night

pan-ya bakery

pasupōto passport

pātii party

pikunikku picnic

Porutogaru Portugal

Porutogaru-go Portuguese (language)

Porutogaru-jin Portuguese (person)

raigetsu next month

rainen next year

raishū next week

raisu rice

rajio radio

reibō-sōchi air conditioner

renkon lotus root

ressha train

resutoran restaurant

retasu lettuce

ringo apple

rippa fine

robii lobby

rōka hall; corridor

rokkā locker

roku six

Roku-gatsu June

Roshia Russia

Roshia-go Russian (language)

Roshia-jin Russian (person)

rūmu room

ryō-gae shimahss exchange money (verb)

ryōji-kan consulate

ryokan inn (traditional)

ryōkin fare

ryokō travel; trip

ryokō-hoken travel insurance

ryokō-sentā travel bureau

ryokō-sha traveler

ryokō shimahss travel (verb)

ryōshū-sho receipt

sā well

sābisu-ryō service charge

saifu wallet

saijitsu national holiday

sakana fish

sakazuki saké cup

sake alcohol; Japanese alcoholic beverage

sakka writer
samui cold (temperature)
samui hi cold day
san three
-san Mr./Mrs./Ms./Miss
San-gatsu March
sanmon temple gate
sanpo walk
sara plate
sarada salad
sarai-nen year after next
sashimi sliced raw fish
Sayōnara. Goodbye.
Seiyō-ryōri Western cuisine
sen one thousand
-sen line (train)
senbei rice cracker
sen-en-satsu 1,000-yen note
sengetsu last month
sensei teacher
sen-senshū week before last
senshū last week
sensō war
sensu folding fan
sentaku suru wash clothes (verb)
Sesshi Celsius
seto-mono pottery
Seto-naikai Inland Sea
shashin photo

shashō conductor (train)
shawā shower
shi four
shiai game; match; tournament
shibaraku moment; awhile
shichi seven
Shichi-gatsu July
Shi-gatsu April
shigoto occupation; work
shiitake type of mushroom
shika deer
shikakui square
shimasen doesn't do; don't do
shimashita did
shimahss do (verb)
shimemahss close (verb)
shinai-denwa local telephone call
shinai-kankō tour of a city
shinbun newspaper
shingō signal
shinguru-rūmu single room
shinju pearl
Shinjuku (place name in Tokyo)
Shinkansen bullet train
shippō-yaki cloisonné
shiro castle
shiseki historical site
shita down
shitei-seki reserved seat

shōchū distilled spirit usually drunk with water or a mixer
shōji paper sliding door
shokubutsu-en botanical garden
shokudō dining hall
shokudō-sha dining car
shokuji meal
shokuji-tsuki meal included
shoppai salty
shūgō-jikan meeting time
shūjitsu weekday
shūmatsu weekend
shumi hobby; interest
shuppatsu-jikan departure time
sō so
soba buckwheat noodles (dark and thin)
soba nearby
sōbetsu-kai farewell party
Sō dess. That's right.
sono that
sore that (pronoun)
sōshiki funeral
soto out; outside
subarashii wonderful
sugu right away
suiden rice paddy
suika watermelon
sui-mono soup (Japanese)
Sui-yōbi Wednesday

suki like
suki-yaki Japanese dish of meat, vegetable, bean curd, etc.
sumi-e Indian-ink painting
Sumimasen. Excuse me.
Sumimasen ga... Sorry, but...
sumō sumo (traditional Japanese wrestling)
sumoggu smog
Supein Spain
Supein-go Spanish (language)
Supein-jin Spanish (person)
supōtsu sport
suppai sour
sūpu soup (Western)
supūn spoon
sushi sushi
sutajiamu stadium
sutēki steak
suzushii cool

tabemahss eat (verb)
Tai Thailand
taifū typhoon
Tai-go Thai (language)
Taihei-yō Pacific Ocean
Tai-jin Thai (person)
taion-kei thermometer
taishi-kan embassy

takai expenive

takenoko bamboo shoot

tako octopus

takusan many; much

takushii-noriba taxi stand

tamago egg

tamanegi onion

tanjō-bi birthday

tasukemahss help (verb)

Tasukete! Help!

te hand

tearai restroom

tegami letter

Teikoku Hoteru Imperial Hotel

teishoku set meal

te-nimotsu ichiji azukari-jo baggage checkroom

tenki weather

tenki-yohō weather forecast

tenpura tempura (Japanese deepfried food)

tenran-kai exhibition

tera Buddhist temple

terebi television

terefon-kādo telephone card

tō pagoda; tower

tō ten (objects)

tōchaku-jikan arrival time

tōfu tofu

tōi far

tōjiki chinaware; ceramics

tōka tenth day of the month

tokei watch; clock

tokei-ya watch shop

tokkuri saké bottle

tokkyū limited express train

tokkyū-ken limited express ticket

Tōkyō Eki Tokyo Station

Tōkyō Tawā Tokyo Tower

tomarimahss stop (a car stops)

tomato tomato

tomemahss stop (a car)

tomodachi friend

tōmorokoshi corn

ton-katsu pork cutlet

toraberāzu-chekku traveler's check

toranku trunk (of a car)

tori bird

torii Shinto shrine archway

torimahss take (verb)

tori-niku chicken

toshi-totta old (not young)

tosho-kan library

totte kudasai please take

tsuā tour

tsugi no hi next day

tsuin twin room

tsuitachi first day of the month

tsuke-mono pickle
tsuki-mi moon viewing
tsumetai cold (to the touch)
tsutsumimahss warp (verb)

udon noodles (white and fat)
ue up
Ueno Kōen Ueno Park
uisukii whiskey
uketori receipt
uketsuke reception
ukiyo-e color print of life in old Japan
umi ocean
una-don broiled eel and rice
unchin fare
unchin-hyō fare table
undō physical exercise
ushiro behind
utsukushii beautiful

wa (subject particle)
wain wine
Wakarimasen. I don't understand.
Wakarimahss. I understand.
warui bad
washi traditional, handmade paper
wasuremahss foreget (verb)
watashi I

yaki-tori grilled, skewered chicken
yakkyoku pharamcy
yakusoku promise; appointment
yakusoku no jikan time set for an
  appointment
yakyū baseball
yakyū no shiai baseball game
yama mountain
yama-nobori mountain climbing
yasai vegetable
yasui inexpensive
yasumi holiday; day off
yattsu eight (objects)
yawarakai soft; tender
yōguruto yogurt
yōka eighth day of the month
yokka fourth day of the month
yoku well
yomimahss read (verb)
yon four
yottsu four (objects)
yoyaku reservation
yūbin de dashimahss mail (a letter)
yūbin-kyoku post office
yūen-chi amusement park
yūgata evening
yuka floor
yukata light, cotton kimono
yuki snow

-yuki bound for
yukkuri slowly
yūmei famous
yu-nomi teacup
yūran-sen excursion boat
zaseki shitei-ken reserved-seat ticket
zasshi magazine
zeikin tax
zō statue